*When the Morning Stars Sang Together*

Nothing is too amazing to be true.

Michael Faraday

Call these fairy tales if you wish to. They all have a
reasonableness that must have originated in some
mighty mind, and better than that, they all tell of the
Indian's faith in the survival of the best impulses of
the human heart, and the ultimate extinction of the
worst.

E. Pauline Johnson, Legends of Vancouver

For ages the army of spirits, once so near, has been
receding further and further from us, banished by the
magic wand of science from hearth and home, from
ruined cell and ivied tower, from haunted glade and
lonely mere, from the riven murky cloud that belches
forth the lightning, and from those fairer clouds that
pillow the silvery moon or fret with flakes of burning
red the golden eve. The spirits are gone even from
their last stronghold in the sky, whose blue arch no
longer passes, except with children, for the screen that
hides from mortal eyes the glories of the celestial
world. Only in poet's dreams or impassionated flights
of oratory is it given to catch a glimpse of the last
flutter of the standards of the retreating host, to hear
the beat of their invisible wings, the sound of their
mocking laughter, or the swell of angel music dying
away in the distance.

J.G. Frazer, The Golden Bough

# When the Morning Stars Sang Together

John S. Morgan

THE BOOK SOCIETY OF CANADA LIMITED
*Agincourt, Canada*

ISBN 0-7725-5079-4 (soft cover)

ISBN 0-7725-5080-8 (case bound)

Design / Peter Maher

Typesetting / E.C.S.

Printer / Alger Press

Manufactured in Canada

# The Artists

JACKSON BEARDY, or ⴑⲘⵉⵏ ⴾⵉⵙⵏⵊ, as he signs his paintings, is a Cree Indian. He was born on the Island Lake reserve, northern Manitoba. After graduating from high school, he completed a course in commercial art at Tech Voc, Winnipeg, and worked in the art department of Simpsons-Sears. After this, he attended the University of Manitoba School of Fine Arts.

Jackson Beardy made a major contribution to the "Indians of Canada Pavilion", Expo '67, which was awarded a Centennial Medal. His work has been exhibited at the National Arts Centre, Ottawa, and also at the Winnipeg Art Gallery. He has been a field researcher for the Manitoba Museum of Man and Nature, taught at the University of Brandon, and conducted classes in art and Indian legends in rural Manitoba and in Winnipeg.

"It has become my deep, personal life goal," he writes, "to create an awareness of our cultural heritage within the public at large, thereby cementing stronger ties of mutual understanding for one country—one Canada."

RON HAMILTON has three Indian names, each of which is important to him: Hupquatchew, from his mother's ancestors; Quay-iss, which is Indian for "He feeds the people"; and Kwa-weena, which in the language of his father's ancestors, the Fort Rupert people, means "Raven".

He belongs to the Opetchesaht tribe from the west coast of Vancouver Island, and was raised on the Ahaswinis Indian reserve. He attended school in Alberni, Terrace, Campbell River and Victoria. For the past two years, he has been assistant carver to Henry Hunt at the Provincial Museum in Victoria.

"It is my life's dream," Ron Hamilton writes, "to be able to move back home and build a cedar plank "big house" of the type my own people used to use. Nothing would make me happier than to see our people use the house for feasts and potlatches, the way these houses should be used; to teach respect for life, and to pass on the customs and history of the people."

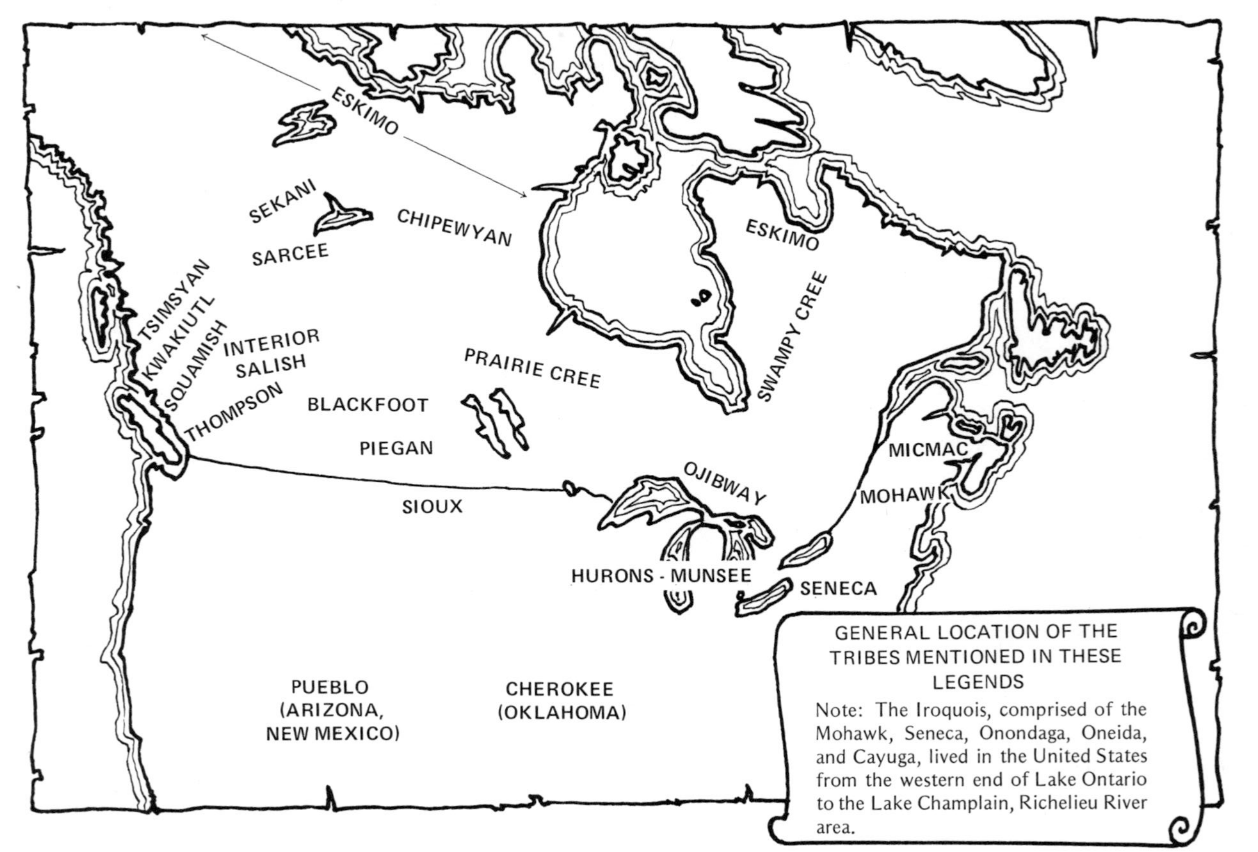

ESKIMO
SEKANI
CHIPEWYAN
SARCEE
ESKIMO
SWAMPY CREE
TSIMSYAN
KWAKIUTL
SQUAMISH
INTERIOR SALISH
THOMPSON
PRAIRIE CREE
BLACKFOOT
PIEGAN
MICMAC
MOHAWK
OJIBWAY
SIOUX
HURONS - MUNSEE
SENECA
GENERAL LOCATION OF THE TRIBES MENTIONED IN THESE LEGENDS
Note: The Iroquois, comprised of the Mohawk, Seneca, Onondaga, Oneida, and Cayuga, lived in the United States from the western end of Lake Ontario to the Lake Champlain, Richelieu River area.
PUEBLO (ARIZONA, NEW MEXICO)
CHEROKEE (OKLAHOMA)

# Contents

# Foreword

An Indian looks at nature and sees beauty—the
woods, the marshes, the mountains, the grasses and
berries, the moose and the field mouse, the soaring
eagle and the flitting hummingbird, the gaudy flowers
and the succulent bulbs. He sees an overall fitness, an
overall collective beauty, but he looks deeper. He sees
the beauty of the individual components of the big
picture. He sees the diversity of the various elements
of the entire scene. He admires the grace of a leaping
deer, the straight-line simplicity of the pines the deer
leaps through, the jagged three-dimensional thrust
into the sky of the rugged peaks, the quick silver flash
of a trout on the surface of a wind-rippled lake. He
turns a sensitive ear to the faraway eerie wail of the
loon and the nearer snuffling grunt of a bear pawing
at a ground squirrel's den, and he blends them into
the whispering of grasses and the bolder talk of the
tall pines. He feels the touch of wind against his cheek
and the coolness of the mist above the rapids. He
surveys the diversities of nature and finds them good.

An Indian thinks this might be the way of people.
He knows that whites and Indians are different. He
knows that there are differences even within these
larger groups, differences between Scot and
Ukrainian, between Cree and Iroquois. He knows
there are differences between man and his brother,
red or white.

To the Indian this is the natural way of things, the
way things should be, as it is in nature.

Harold Cardinal, The Unjust Society

For the Indian, the number four possessed magic
properties. Four days and four nights, he prepared
himself to communicate with his god; four fires blazed
at the great lodge during the ceremonies of the Tloo-

qwah-nah;[1] his songs were sung four times; when an Indian child had heard a legend or a story four times, he was expected to have grasped its main idea.

Appropriately then, behind the writing of this book were four purposes. The prime purpose was to encourage the reader, through legend, to discover the culture and heritage of the North American Indian.

A second purpose was to show that the literature of the native people illustrates a way of life that is, in many respects, in direct contrast with that of the white man. This way of life can best be described by the term *involvement*. From early childhood, the Indian was encouraged to become involved, to play a part in the activities of his tribe. This is shown in the potlatch. Young boys packed the wood indoors in preparation for the coming events, hunters provided the game from the forest, young men carried the carcasses down to the lodges, the women and the older men prepared them for eating. Parents proudly watched their offspring when they were called upon to participate in a play.[2] Here was no generation gap, no isolation of the individual. In a larger dimension, the Indian felt a sense of kinship to the world of nature. In fact, he was one with his community, one with his tribe, and one with nature.[3]

A third purpose was to show the narrative excellence of the Indian legends.[4] These have the qualities of any good short story. Their themes are eternal: love, courage, sacrifice, the quest for the elusive or the unattainable.

A fourth purpose in writing the book was to draw some of the parallels between the ancient Greek and the North American Indian stories. In doing so, I have concentrated upon those legends which have exerted a strong influence upon English literature—the Greek classical legends.

No attempt has been made in this book to account for these underlying similarities; rather, the reader has been left to form his own conclusions.[5]

1. This was called the "potlatch" by the white man, probably because the Nootka verb *pa-chitte*, "to give", was heard so often in the ceremony. See George Clutesi, *Potlatch*, Gray's Publishing Ltd.
2. George Clutesi, *Potlatch*
3. This is true of most early communities: "Members of the pre-civilized community had a strong sense of group solidarity. No doubt they thought of themselves as naturally belonging together, and so far as they were aware of people different from themselves they thought their own ways better than the ways of others. . . . The disposition to see what is around one as human and personal like oneself is not, in pre-civilized or primitive society, limited to people; a great deal of what we regard as nature is so regarded". Robert Redfield, *The Primitive World and Its Transformations*, Cornell University Press
4. Both legends and myths may be classified under the term "folklore". Legends are improbable or fanciful stories handed down from the past by word of mouth. A legend often begins with a fact—with a significant event or the exploits of a notable person. It is told and retold, until, in the course of time, it is exaggerated—often distorted beyond recognition. A myth is an attempt to give meaning to the universe. Myths deal, not with real events or people, but with supernatural events or characters, with a world order believed to have preceded the present one. Legends frequently predate myths. When legends are incorporated into the adventures of some god or are accorded some religious significance, they become myths.
5. The history of the various schools of thought on this subject has been presented by Richard Dorson in *The British Folklorists*, University of Chicago Press. More controversial explanations are provided by Immanuel Velikovsky in *Worlds in Collision*, Doubleday Publishers, and by Erich von Daniken in *Chariots of the Gods*, Souvenir Press.

# Acknowledgements

We wish to thank the following authors (or their representatives) who have kindly permitted the reproduction of copyright material.

The Chilton Book Company: "Hiawatha and Atotarho", adapted from *Our Indian Heritage: Profiles of 12 Great Leaders*, C. Fayne Porter. Copyright © 1964 by the author. Used with the permission of the publisher, Chilton Book Company, Radnor, Pennsylvania. Clarke, Irwin & Company Ltd.: excerpt from *Growing Pains* and from *Klee Wyck*, Emily Carr; excerpt from "Interval with Halycons", *The Net and the Sword*, Douglas LePan. Clay, Charles: "Wesukechak and the Loon", adapted from *Swampy Cree Legends*, Macmillan Company of Canada Ltd. Colonial Printers Limited: "The Enchanted Bear", adapted from *History and Folklore of the Cowichan Indians*, Martha D. Harris. Cornell University Press: excerpt reprinted from *The Primitive World and Its Transformations*, Robert Redfield. Copyright © 1953 by Cornell University. Used by permission of Cornell University Press. Crown Publishers, Inc.: excerpt from *A Pictorial History of the American Indian*, Oliver La Farge. Copyright © 1956 by Oliver La Farge and Crown Publishers, Inc. Gage Educational Publishing Limited: reprints of "The Loon's Necklace" and "The River of Whispering Ghosts", *Native Tribes of Canada*, Dr. Douglas Leechman. Gyldenal: "The Story of Sedna", adapted from *Eskimo Folk-Tales*, Knud Rasmussen & W. Worster. The Hamlyn Publishing Group (Canada) Ltd.: "Hinun, the Giant of Niagara Falls", adapted from *American Indian Tales and Legends*, Vladimir Hulpach; "The Pueblo Indian Story of the Creation of the World", adapted from *North American Indian Mythology*, Cottie Burland. Harper & Row, Inc.: excerpt 'Those who dwell . . . spring after winter' from pp. 88-9 *The Sense of Wonder*, Rachel L. Carson, copyright © 1956 by Rachel L. Carson. Hodder & Stoughton Ltd.: "The Pilot of the Plains", *Flint and Feather*, E. Pauline Johnson. Hogarth Press: excerpt from *The Dark Eye in Africa* and from *The Lost World of the Kalahari*, Laurens van der Post. Hurtig Publishers: excerpt from *The Unjust Society*, Harold Cardinal. Information Canada: "The Corn Goddess", adapted from "The Corn Goddess", Diamond Jenness (bulletin 141, National Museums of Canada); "The Strong Man of the Tsimsyan Legends", adapted from "Tsimsyan Myths", Marius Barbeau (bulletin 174, National Museums of Canada). Source: The National Museum of Man of The National Museums of Canada. Reproduction authorized by Information Canada. McClelland & Stewart Ltd.: excerpt from *Indian Legends of Canada*, Ella Elizabeth Clark, and for adaptations of the following legends from it, "Coyote and the salmon", "The boy's vigil and the first robin", "The first white water lily", "A legend of Siwash rock", "The origin of the sun dance" ("The North Star"), "The spirit sacrifice", "The story of Lone Bird, the woman in the moon". Excerpt from *Legends of Vancouver*, E. Pauline Johnson, and for adaptations of the following legends from it, "Deadman's Island", ("The First Fire-Flowers"), "The Deep Waters", "The Lost Island", "The Lure in Stanley Park" ("The Cathedral Trees of Stanley Park"), "The Two Sisters" ("The Legend of the Twin Sisters"). Macmillan Company of Canada Ltd.: excerpts from *The Golden Bough*, J.G. Frazer. McGraw-Hill Ryerson Limited: "Two Dead Persons", adapted from *Legends of My People, the Great Ojibway*, Norval Morriseau. Oxford University Press (Canadian Branch): "The Boy in the Land of Shadows", "How the Birds Got Their Colours", adapted from *Glooskap's Country and Other Indian Tales* (1956), Cyrus Macmillan. Tales first published by John Lane, The Bodley Head, Limited, in *Canadian Wonder Tales* (1918), and *Canadian Fairy Tales* (1922); "The Legend of the Wishing Well" and "The Sleeping Giant", adapted from *Thunder in the Mountains*, Hilda Mary Hooke. Oxford University Press (New York): excerpts from *The Sea Around Us*, Rachel L. Carson. University of Oklahoma Press: excerpt from *Sequoyah*, Grant Foreman. Copyright © 1938 by the University of Oklahoma Press. A.P. Watt & Sons: excerpt from *The Greek Myths: I and II*, Robert Graves. Penguin Books Ltd.

Every reasonable effort has been made to trace ownership of copyright material. Information will be welcomed which will enable the publisher to rectify any reference in future printing.

# Introduction

The legends of the North American Indian reflect the awe, the sense of wonder that he felt when he beheld the handiwork of the Creator. To him, there were no inanimate objects. He was "acutely aware of the forces of growth pounding through the forest, aware of the sap gushing in every leaf, of push, push, push, the bursting of buds, the creeping of vines".[1] Nature was not something "out there"; it was a part, or an extension, of himself. He peopled it with supernatural beings, with animals that talked and behaved like humans, and, indeed, often became human. His trees spoke of the glories of the past; in some cases, in an earlier existence, they had been human.

We who live in Canada do not need to journey far to become infused with the magic of the Indian's world. It is everywhere around us. As I drive along the road leading to the Indian reservation of Parry Island, I am mindful of the story of Kitchikewana, who picked up the thirty thousand islands of Georgian Bay, and flung them, helter-skelter, into the places they have occupied ever since. Exhausted by his herculean task, Kitchikewana lay down and passed away to the

Spirit World. His body was so huge that the Indians could not remove it for burial. Gathering from far and near, they covered the gigantic corpse with sand and rocks, thus forming the long hill still known as the "Giant's Tomb".[2]

Everything in nature—trees and flowers, birds and animals, the moon and the stars—has a story to tell. The trees, whether decked in autumnal splendour or cloaked in the fresh green of spring, remind us of the purpose of their creation: Manitou could not stoop low enough to touch the flowers, so he made the trees. Many legends offer an explanation of their fall colours. Most of these are concerned with the "Giant of the North". One legend, however, states that Nanna Bijou, having stolen fire from the giant who guarded it, set a field ablaze to cover his escape. The leaves of the trees reflected the red, gold, yellow, and bronze of Nanna Bijou's fire. This so intrigued him that he decided to change them into these shades in the autumn of every year.[3] The autumn mist that rises from the marsh and lowland and veils the bright foliage is the smoke from the campfire of Glooscap, the benevolent deity of the Micmacs.

The fire-flowers that crowd the margins of our lanes and byways were once valiant warriors who sacrificed their lives that others might live.[4] The water lily that looks up at us as we paddle past is a star fallen from heaven.[5] The birds of the forest were created by Glooscap from the multihued leaves as they lay on the ground, stricken by the Giant of the North.[6] To this day, they prefer to dwell on high, amongst the foliage from which they were made. The loon, messenger of Glooscap, swims up and down the inland northern waterways, calling for his master, who has, long ago, departed to the land of eternal summer.

At night, the moon turns the lakes to silver, and

stars bejewel the sky. These, too, have their stories. Indian legend tells of the woman who, having fallen in love with the moon, was taken up into the sky to dwell.[7] The Milky Way is the snow shaken from the cloak of Wakinu, the gray bear, as he crossed the Bridge of Dead Souls on his way to the Eternal Hunting Grounds.[8] The Pleiades were seven poor boys who, having known nothing but hunger and cold in this world, were changed into stars.[9]

Most of the legends testify to the qualities which the Indian admired and cherished: courage, self-sacrifice, generosity, resourcefulness. They exemplify, as well, the Indian's humility, his realization that there exists "a power that shapes our ends"; his awareness of the splendour of nature; his power of projecting his personality into (and so fully comprehending) the world of nature around him.

A number of Indian legends are of a comic nature, a product of his sense of fun and his delight in the ludicrous. These usually involve a "trickster", a demigod, who was not only the instigator of the trickery, but often its unwilling recipient, as well. He appears in the legends of most Indian tribes: Wesukechak of the Cree, Napi of the Blackfoot, Crow of the Kutchin, Coyote of the Western Plateau tribes, Raven of the Pacific coast tribes, and others.

I am very grateful for the suggestions given by the Department of Indian Affairs and Northern Development. I also wish to thank those members of the Department of Education, Manitoba, who offered helpful comments.

*John S. Morgan*

1. Emily Carr, *Growing Pains*. Clarke, Irwin & Company Ltd.
2. Hugh F. Dent, "Under the Stars", *The North Star*, Parry Sound
3. Dorothy M. Reid, *Tales of Nanabozho*. Oxford University Press
4. E. Pauline Johnson, *Legends of Vancouver*. McClelland & Stewart Ltd.
5. a Chippewa (Ojibway) legend
6. Cyrus MacMillan, *Glooskap's Country and Other Indian Tales*. Oxford University Press
7. a Chippewa (Ojibway) legend
8. Vladimir Hulpach, *American Indian Tales and Legends*. The Hamlyn Publishing Group (Canada) Ltd.
9. Assiniboine and Blackfoot legend; see Vladimir Hulpach, *American Indian Tales and Legends*

# 1
# When the Morning Stars Sang Together

> Where were you when I laid the foundations of the
> earth? Tell me if you have understanding. Who
> determined its measurements—surely you know!
> Or who stretched the line upon it? Or where were
> its bases sunk, or who laid its cornerstone, when the
> morning stars sang together, and all the sons of God
> sang for joy?
> Or who shut in the sea with doors, when it burst
> forth from the womb; when I made clouds its
> garment, and thick darkness its swaddling band?
>
> *Job XXXVIII: 4-8*

Early man, conscious of his frailties before the
strength of the animals, the whims of the elements,
the violence of natural upheavals, was aware also of
his insignificance before the power and glory of a
Being far greater than himself—a Being who must have
laid the foundations of the universe;[1]

---

1. Many believe that the belief in one god did not come in one
   illuminating flash, but was the result of a progression from
   animism, the attributing of an innate soul to natural phenomena, to the belief in many gods.

> When I look at the heavens, the works of thy fingers,
> the moon and the stars which thou hast established;
> What is man that thou art mindful of him,
> And the son of man that thou dost care for him?
>
> *Psalms VIII:3-4*

From an awareness of a Power behind the universe, the logical query is: When and how were the world's foundations laid? When did life begin? How was man created? The Greek explanation is similar to the Biblical; i.e., order grew out of disorder: "In the beginning the world was without form and void, and darkness was upon the face of the deep; and the Spirit of God was moving over the face of the waters."[2]

The Greeks conceived of the earth and the firmament emerging from an amorphous mass. After eons of Chaos, were created the Earth-Mother (broad-bosomed Gaia), the unshaken habitation of the deathless gods; dark Tartarus, within the depths of Earth; and Love (Eros), fairest among the immortal gods. Later from Chaos two gigantic forms loomed forth: the Goddess Night and her brother Erebus, the Depth. And Gaia bore Uranus, the Heaven or Firmament, that he might cover her utterly about.[3] Thus the Earth and the Firmament arose out of Chaos.

Since the Greeks saw everywhere about them life springing from the Earth as a result of the beneficent touch of the Sun, so Gaia, the Earth-Mother, and Uranus, the Sky-Father, united to produce new life: first the powerful and beautiful Titans, amongst whom was Cronus, father of the mighty Zeus, who eventually seized control of the Universe; then huge wheel-eyed creatures called Cyclopes; and finally three mighty sons, each with a hundred arms and fifty heads growing from his shoulders.[4]

The Indians' explanation of the Earth's origin differs from that of the Greeks' in that animals play the significant role. This reflects the kinship that the Indians felt towards the animal world, although the later Indian myths, such as the following Pueblo account of creation, tend to magnify the role of man.

## The Pueblo Indian Story of the Creation of the World

Since the beginning was Awonawilona, "the one who contains everything". Otherwise, all was utter blackness and nothingness. Then from Awonawilona the mists of increasing and the streams of growing flowed. Awonawilona assumed form and out of darkness fashioned the great light, the Sun. As the Sun touched the mists, they were gathered together to form raindrops which became the sea whereon the world floats.

Then Awonawilona planted his seed on the waters. Upon the warm caress of the Sun the seed was nourished and grew to form a green scum that gathered over the waters, increasing until it became solid. Then it was divided to become two: the Earth-Mother and the Firmament, or Sky-Father, who covers everything.

2. Genesis I:2

3. 4

   *Hesiod, "Theogony", Poems and Fragments,* tr. A.W. Mair. Oxford University Press

The Sky-Father joined with the Earth-Mother and life took form within her. Then she spat on the water and stirred it with her fingers until a foam arose.[5] She breathed upon the foam and created mists and rainbows which floated as clouds above the sea. The Sky-Father breathed and cool, life-giving rain fell from the clouds.

Then the Sky-Father held out his hand, which contained grains of shining maize—some silver, some gold—numerous as the sands of the desert. The silver grains, he flung at the sky and they became the stars, the lesser lights of the firmament. The gold, he gently placed in the clefts of the breasts of Mother-Earth saying, "These golden grains shall be the food for our children."

The Sky-Father and the Earth-Mother then separated. Life quickened within Mother-Earth. However, the first creatures were deformed and monstrous, writhing hideously as they sought to emerge from the dark womb of Earth into the light of day; but, with the passing of time, their ugliness dropped from them and they assumed shapes resembling men and women. Of these myriad creatures, only one, Poshaiyangkyo, whose name means "One Alone", was able to escape from the depths of Earth. Emerging into the blessed day, he prayed for the release of his brothers and sisters who were still struggling for the light.

In answer, the Sky-Father cast his seed on the foam around the earth and the foam gave birth to the twins, Preceder and Follower. Immediately, they hurled their mighty thunderbolts and cleft the earth. Then the twins descended the dark chasm to release the others. Binding grass, vines, and trees together, they formed a living ladder to enable the imprisoned to emerge from the depths. Some slipped and, with hideous screams, fell back into the enveloping darkness, later to be spewed up by Earth in the form of dreadful monsters that roamed the earth when it was young. However the fittest survived and emerged into the upper world.

Here, once their eyes became accustomed to the light, they shrank with terror. Unearthly screams and groans rent the air as they beheld the monstrous, scaly, slimy creatures that crept and writhed over the barren, rocky surfaces broken only by volcanoes that loomed before them. Trembling, they sank to the ground, praying to the Sky-Father for deliverance.

Hearing the pleas of his children, Sky-Father was moved to immediate action. Thunderbolt after thunderbolt, he hurled earthward. His terrified children cowered under whatever shelter they could find, while the earth trembled and shook before the mighty assault from on high.

Then peace descended like a dove. The people looked round about them and saw that the monsters had been destroyed, and that the earth, broken and furrowed, was ready for the first seeds.

To this day, one can sometimes see the bones of these monstrous inhabitants of our early earth and, in the scorched rocks, the reminder of the might of Sky-Father.

The next legend, the Iroquois' and Hurons' explanation of the origin of the world, in all likelihood had its beginnings in an early period of their history, before they had begun to cultivate the soil and when they were dependent entirely on hunting and fishing for sustenance. They were in close communion with the creatures of the forest. Every day they witnessed

5. In Greek mythology, Aphrodite was born from the foam of the sea.

the cunning, ferocity, strength, and fleetness of the animals. Hence they tended to put them on an equal, if not a superior, level with themselves, as the following legend illustrates.


## How the World Began

Far, far above us, dwell the people of the sky. They are like us, only taller, more erect, more beautiful and noble in countenance and bearing. Their faces are placid and friendly, unscarred by wounds and unwrinkled by age; for, dwelling in the sky world and living in peace, they know neither the scourge of time nor the cruel hand of war. Like us, they live in lodges, are clothed in the robes of bear and wolf, and hunt for the animals of field and forest which abound everywhere in this happy land. If you look skyward on a clear night, you will see the light from the sky world peeping through the floor of the sky. We call these peepholes stars.

At one time, below this sky world, there was only the wide sea stretching forever. There were no people; only the animals that dwelt in the sea: toad, beaver, muskrat, fish, turtle, and the birds of the sea.

Then, one day, down from the sky world a woman fell.[6] Observing this, and fearing lest she drown in the vast depths of the sea, two loons[7] spread their wings together and formed a cushion to break her fall.

6. The star woman was pregnant when she was forced from the upper world.
7. The loons appear in many Indian legends. In the Micmac cycle they are Glooscap's messengers. Their lonely, haunting cry is vividly depicted in Lampman's poem "The Loons"

   And now, though many alternating years
   Have passed among the desolate northern mires

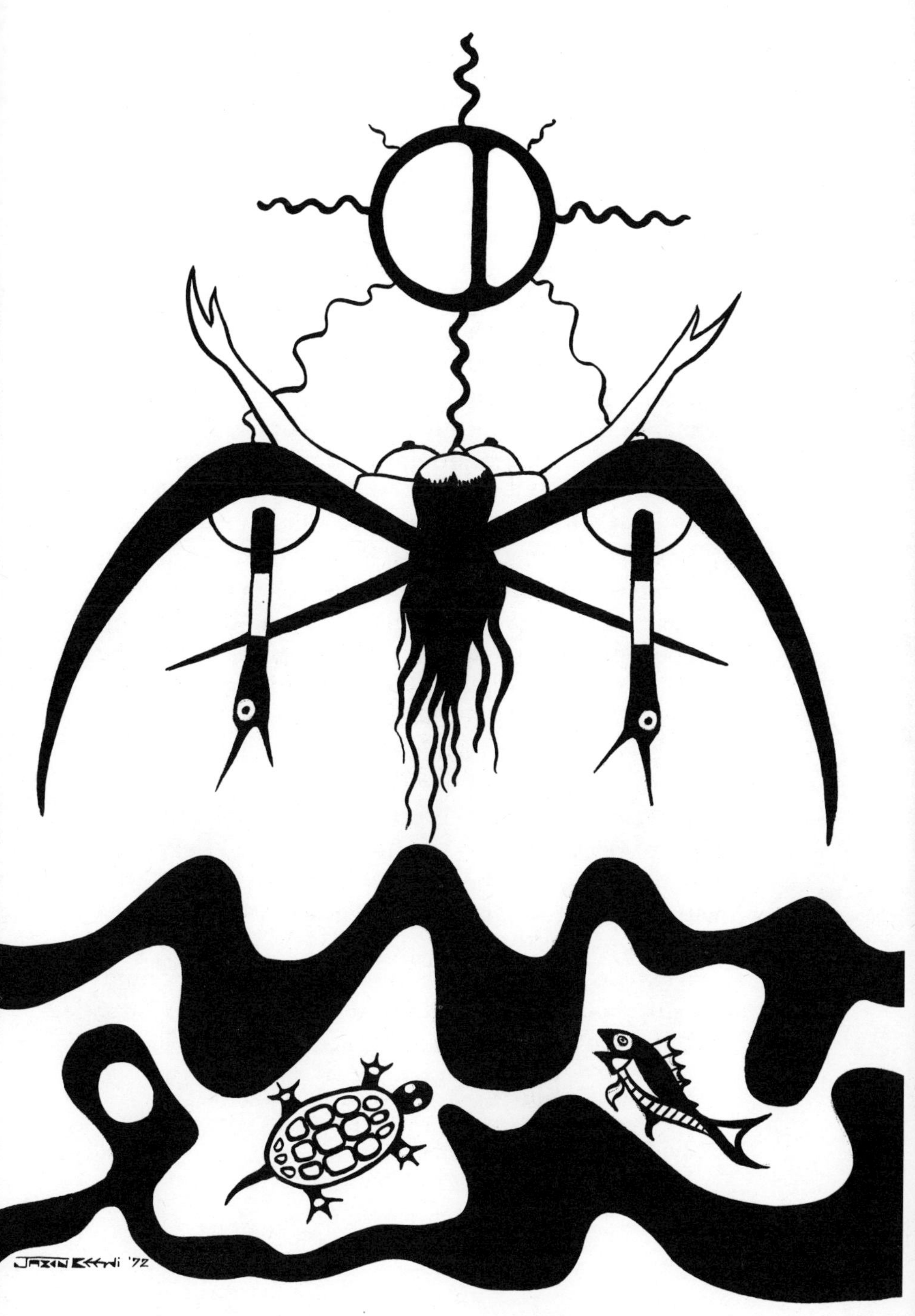

The loons called to the other animals for help, their cries rising, falling, then gradually disappearing in the endless waters. Great Turtle heard their wailing notes, and, gathering other creatures to him, came to the rescue.

"My back is broad," he said. "Let me take her." Thus he relieved the loons of their heavy burden.

As you know, Great Turtle, who now carries the world on his back, is endowed with many strange and wonderful powers. He knew that the woman and her offspring needed earth if they were to live. However, although Great Turtle has the power to make larger whatever exists, he cannot create anything. Therefore, knowing that somewhere in the depths of the waters there was mud, he called on Beaver to dive to the bottom of the sea and bring some mud to the surface.

Beaver, realizing the depth he would be required to dive, at first objected. Then, urged on by Great Turtle, he agreed to try. Down he plunged; deeper and deeper, he descended until he disappeared from the sight of Great Turtle and his companions, who were peering anxiously into the water. At first, bubbles of air broke its surface, but, after a few minutes, the undisturbed expanse gave no indication of life.

Just as they had given up hope, the almost lifeless form of Beaver rose to the surface. He had risked his life to carry out the wishes of Great Turtle, but without success. His paws gave no evidence of the slightest particle of mud.

Next Great Turtle sent Muskrat in search of mud. He also could find no end to the waters. Then Toad asked if he could try. Great Turtle refused. He was

> Still must you search and wander querulously,
> Crying for Glooscap, still bemoan the light
> With weird entreaties, and in agony
> With awful laughter pierce the lonely light.

sure that, as Beaver and Muskrat had failed, this small creature would have no chance. But Toad insisted, and, more in weariness than consent, Great Turtle relented. Joyfully, Toad dived into the waters, which almost immediately swallowed him up. Time dragged on. The bubbles had long ceased to rise to the surface. The loons and Beaver, who had now recovered, looked at Great Turtle and shook their heads.

Despairing, they were about to turn away when they saw the limp body of Toad floating on the water some distance from where he had disappeared. Gently, they lifted him out and, behold, within his lifeless mouth, Great Turtle saw some mud. Sadly he handed this to the woman, who placed it carefully on the edge of a shell. Gradually it spread, unevenly in places, forming dips and mounds which grew larger and larger until mountains and valleys were formed.[8] Soon the world took shape, and was ready for trees and plants and animals.

Then the woman gave birth to twins: Glooscap and Malsumsis. These twins were of exactly opposite natures and had quarrelled, even in their mother's womb. Malsumsis, refusing to be born in the ordinary way, broke forth from his mother's side and killed her. Where she lay, the earth grew rich: pumpkin vines spread their tendrils from her eyes, golden maize grew from her breasts, and shoots of beans rose from where her limbs had been. All these plants grew and multiplied in the now fertile earth.

8. Variations of this story appear in the legends of different tribes. The account of soil being formed on the back of the turtle occurs also in Micmac and Malecite legends. In the Cree version, Wesukechak told the snakes to make rivers. The wolf pushed big piles of mud with his nose to create mountains and formed lakes by jumping about in the soft earth with his big feet.

The power of Malsumsis spread throughout the land. To plague man, he created fierce animals such as the wolf, the bear, and the panther, as well as enormous mosquitoes and flies. He formed a gigantic toad that drank up all the fresh water and threatened man's very existence by drought. On the other hand, Glooscap created animals to help man: the dog as his companion; the elk, deer, caribou, turkey, and partridge as his supply of food; the birds of the forest as his source of beauty.

Later Glooscap invaded the territory of Malsumsis. Everywhere, he was met by gigantic snakes, fierce beasts, and huge mosquitoes. Although he could not destroy them, he had the power to make them smaller so that man would be capable of mastering them. In the final encounter between the brothers, Glooscap slew the wicked Malsumsis, who after death retreated to the West where he awaits us all.

Thus, the earth, man, and living creatures, good and bad, were formed.

The greatest mystery of life is life itself. Modern medicine has accomplished many wonders. It can prolong life by the use of wonder drugs, heart transplants, and other operations. Some scientists predict that life may be preserved hundreds of years by a freezing process. However, strive as he may, man has been unable to penetrate the ultimate mystery—the *creation* of life.

Therefore it is little wonder that primitive peoples bowed down before the sources of life: the earth, the sun, and the sea.

Since, in the human species, woman is the fount of life, it was natural for primitive peoples to identify her with her counterparts in the world around her: the earth, the sun, and the sea.

We have seen how the Indians related her to the earth in both the creation myth of the Pueblo Indians and that of the Iroquois and Hurons. Similarly, with the Greeks, the earth was a goddess, as was Demeter, sister of Zeus, in whose care were the germination of seeds and the growth of plants. Without her, as the following story testifies, life on earth would come to an end.

## Demeter and Persephone

The childhood of the earth, as childhood should be, was a happy, carefree time. Both men and animals dwelt in peace, wars were unknown; and man, by the sweat of his brow, was not forced to eke a meagre living from a stubborn soil. The earth yielded plentiful crops all the year round, for there were no seasons as we know them today. Amidst this happy scene, surrounded by the abundance that she had created, dwelt Demeter, the goddess of the corn, and her daughter, Persephone, radiant as the sunrise.

However happiness is like a flower: it blooms but for a moment and then is gone forever. Hades, dark god of the Underworld, lonely in his realm of the dead, beheld Persephone in her radiance and beauty and longed to have her. Leaving his kingdom of the dead, he petitioned his brother Zeus for her hand. Zeus, the cloud-gatherer, the king of the gods, fearful of arousing the wrath of Demeter, at first refused Hades. But when Hades persisted in his entreaties, Zeus said, tactfully, that though he would not give his consent, neither would he withhold it.

This was all Hades needed to complete his plans for abducting Persephone. One day, seeing a meadow full of fragrant poppies swaying in the breeze, Persephone left her companions. Just as she was about to pluck a blossom, a chasm opened in the earth and a chariot, drawn by four black horses and driven by a charioteer (Hades) whose face was invisible, loomed before the terrified girl. Hades clasped his strong arm about her. The earth closed behind her and the cold darkness of the nether world engulfed her. Her screams rent the air, but to no avail. While her companions frolicked in a nearby meadow, Persephone had been swallowed by the earth.

On discovering Persephone's absence, Demeter, holding a flaming torch in each hand, searched frantically for her child day and night. The only information she could obtain was from Hecate, the goddess of Night. She had heard the girl's screams, but on hurrying to the scene, had found no trace of her.

Despairing of success and broken with grief, Demeter shunned the race of man. Suspecting Zeus's complicity in a plot against her, she forsook the councils of the gods and refused to help man. The trees no longer yielded fruit and the plants withered and died in the barren soil.

Fearing that mankind would be destroyed utterly, Zeus sent Iris, the rainbow goddess, to plead with Demeter to relent and return to the councils of the gods. But Demeter remained adamant: until her daughter was restored to her, the earth would remain barren.

Realizing that no other course was open, Zeus yielded and despatched Hermes, the winged messenger of the gods, to Hades. Reluctantly, Hades was forced to accede to Zeus's command and return Persephone to her mother.

Just as the eager Persephone was about to mount Hermes's chariot, Hades plucked a pomegranate from a nearby tree. The unsuspecting girl took it. Then quickly she was borne out of the pit of darkness into the realm of light, and joyful was her reunion with her mother.

Soon a dark cloud threatened to obscure the happiness of their reunion. The wily Hades now claimed that Persephone had partaken of food in the abode of the dead, to which, therefore, she must return. Demeter retaliated with her previous threat—"Unless my child is restored to me the earth will remain barren: the trees will bear no fruit, the plants will cease to grow, and the race of man will perish."

Then Zeus reached a decision that was acceptable to all. Persephone would spend three months of the year with Hades in the Underworld; the remainder of the year, she would abide with her mother on earth.

Therefore, for the three months that Persephone is in Hades, Demeter neglects the earth. It becomes cold and barren, the trees and plants wither and lose their leaves. But, in the spring, Persephone returns and all nature sings. The brooks flow; the birds, Persephone's messengers, bring tidings of her coming; life stirs within plants and trees. As the season advances, the trees deck themselves in leafy glory and the birds wear their finest feathers. Then autumn arrives and honours Persephone with its gifts of the harvest; but, alas, it brings, too, a reminder that soon she must return to the land of the dead.

## The Corn Goddess

The story of Gosadaya, the great hunter, and the Corn Goddess is the Iroquois counterpart of the Greek story of Demeter and her daughter Persephone.

One day, long, long ago, the mighty hunter, Gosadaya, left the lodges of his people to seek the wildernesses and the solitary places, for he wished to talk to the Great Spirit, and only after one is far removed from the company of others in the silence of the forest does the Great Spirit listen to the voices of his children. When he had climbed to the top of a high hill that looked down on the distant forest, Gosadaya built a lodge for fasting. Here he fasted for seven days and seven nights before lifting his voice to the Great Spirit in prayer.

When he prayed, he prayed not for himself by asking for greater skill in hunting or for greater craft in fishing; but for his people, that they might be granted a source of life more dependable than the animals of the forest, the fish of the streams, the berries, and the wild rice that grows in the marshy places.

A few nights later, on his homeward journey, as he lay sleeping by the fire, Gosadaya was wakened by a rustling like the stir of shadows in the flickering firelight. Then out of the shadows stepped a slim, beautiful Indian maiden, dressed in garments of green and yellow. In the light of the fire, her hair shone. She spoke to Gosadaya in a voice that was gentle and low.

"The Great Spirit has listened to your prayers. Since I am to be the means by which your prayers will be answered, he has sent me to marry you."

"The Great Spirit has spoken; therefore, it shall be done," replied Gosadaya.

When Gosadaya returned with his wife to the village, his people gathered at his long house to welcome them. Now, at that time, the Indians knew nothing about planting; they lived solely by what nature provided them in the way of game, fish, berries, grapes, and wild rice. The Great Spirit, however, had given Gosadaya's wife the seeds of corn.

She distributed these to the people and showed them how to plant the kernels, making the earth soft and loose above them.

Shortly afterwards the rain came, and then the gentle touch of the sun which warmed the earth. Soon a soft green feather broke through the ground; this was followed by another, then another. Before many days, the maize waved its shining green leaves and yellow tresses in the light breeze.

When the green leaves turned yellow, and the soft, juicy kernels were yellow and hard, Gosadaya's wife showed the people how to harvest the corn, how to strip the husks from the ripened ears, how to make mortars and pestles for grinding the corn, and how to bake it into bread.

At this time, Gosadaya's people were happy and content. They liked the food with which his wife had provided them. Furthermore it seemed to assure them of a more reliable source of life than they had known hitherto.

However, just as the distant voice of thunder drives sullen clouds across the blue sky and causes the sun to seek shelter, so this joyful life was soon to be darkened by unhappiness.

During the absence of Gosadaya on a hunting trip, a younger brother came to visit him. Gosadaya's wife asked him to partake of the new food.

Never having seen bread before, the younger brother looked at it disdainfully and hurled it to the ground, exclaiming, "What is this that you are offering me?"

At this incivility, the woman wept. She was still weeping when Gosadaya returned that night. Sorrowfully, she said to him, "Since your brother has scorned the food, the gift of the Great Spirit, which I have brought you, I can abide with you no longer. If you should wish ever to see me again you must take a long journey towards the rising sun until you come to a big water hole. Here you must lie down to rest. During the night, you will hear the sound of a baby crying. Take an arrow and point it in the direction of the sound. In the morning, walk in this direction."

Whereupon she left his hut and vanished into the shadows of the forest. Just before daylight, the people heard a sound like driving rain. It was the grains dropping from the ears of corn. In the morning, the villagers looked in dismay at the stalks. They now held only ear after ear empty of corn.

Then, from the north, a cold wind rose which spread a cloak of snow over the land and imprisoned rivers and lakes beneath a sheet of ice. Frost held the forest in a silence broken only by the stir of branches now stripped of leaves and the splitting of tree trunks. Gosadaya and the other hunters went into the forest in search of game, but brought back very little. Each day Gosadaya's heart grew heavier with sorrow—sorrow for his lost wife and sorrow for his people whom he saw getting weaker and thinner until they were mere walking skeletons. The plaintive cries of the children bothered him most.

Then, realizing that he could do little here to help his people, he set out in search of his wife. He travelled towards the rising sun until he came to a big water hole. As the sun had just ended its westward journey and the shadows of night were hovering, Gosadaya lit a fire and lay down, exhausted after days of weary travel. About midnight the silence was broken by the crying of a child. Quickly he arose and, with trembling fingers, pointed an arrow on the ground in the direction of the sound. Then he lay down to await the coming of dawn.

No sooner had the fingers of light pushed aside the curtain of darkness than Gosadaya was on his way, travelling in the direction the arrow indicated. However hope gave way to disappointment as he walked all day and still there was no sign of his wife. At night he lit another fire and lay down to rest. This time, however, he did not sleep. He listened to every sound in the breathing forest. About midnight, he heard again the crying of a child, this time closer than before. Again he pointed his arrow in the direction of the sound.

On the third night, he heard a rustling noise and looked up. By the fire, her hair soft and shining and her face radiant as she gazed down upon him, stood his wife.

"I have come to take you back with me," he said, "for my people are starving."

Sorrowfully, she answered, "I can never return to your people, but I shall remain here with you for a time."

True to her word, she lived with Gosadaya for the remainder of the winter. But one day, as the snows were melting and voices of spring filled the land, she said, "Listen!"

From beneath the ground he heard crying.

"They are crying because I have left them," she said. "I can stay with you no longer. However, before I leave, I shall give you some corn to take back to your people."

Whereupon she gave him a bundle containing thousands of small grains of corn, each of which had shrivelled to almost nothing.

For the last time she spoke to him. "When you return, shake this bundle and the grains will regain

their natural size. Have your people plant the grains and care for them as I have instructed, and they shall never hunger. Farewell, dear husband."

She was gone, and he never saw her again.

The next morning Gosadaya began the long journey to his own land. After many days of travel, he reached the village and called his people to the long house, where he shook the bundle until the grains regained their normal size. Then he distributed them to the women to plant. This time, before the seeds were sowed, the people took care to ask the Great Spirit's blessing on their undertaking, and it yielded an abundant harvest.

Gosadaya was happy for his people; yet he longed for his wife. No longer did he share in the festivities and feasts, but, with each passing day, seemed to withdraw more and more into himself. Hour after hour, he would sit motionless, his thoughts far removed from the village life about him. Then one morning he disappeared, and, though they searched everywhere, they could not find him.

Some say that he has found his wife, the corn goddess, in the land beyond the big water hole; others believe that he is searching for her to this day.

## The Woman Who Lives in the Sea

From the evidence of the rocks and the conclusions of geologists, we believe that life began in the sea. Man is a newcomer on the earth, which was about two and a half billion years old before he made his appearance. Thousands of millions of years ago, when the continents were a bleak and barren expanse of rock, void of even the vestiges of life, the first simple form of plant life, the algae, appeared on the surface of the waters. Probably small and soft invertebrates which took their nourishment from the algae were the prototypes of animal life. As life, through millions of years, increased and multiplied, came the first creatures to leave any evidence of their existence in the rocks: the trilobite, the ancient ancestor of the modern crab; the brachiopod, the first type of shell fish; and the sea scorpion, the highest order of life when the world was young. Then, perhaps, as the weeds and plants of the ocean, through the eons, adapted themselves to intertidal conditions, they tentatively encroached upon the land. As life developed, the early dependence on the sea decreased, but, even to this day, there is no form of plant or animal life that does not retain in some manner—in the moisture present in the air it breathes or the food it eats—this dependence on the water from which all life emerged. The body of man gives ample evidence of his watery origin:

> Each of us carries in our veins a salty stream in which the elements sodium, potassium, and calcium are combined in almost the same proportions as in sea water. This is our inheritance from the day, untold millions of years ago, when a remote ancestor, having progressed from the one-celled to the many-celled stage, first developed a circulatory system in which the fluid was merely the water of the sea. In the same way, our lime-hardened skeletons are a heritage from the calcium-rich oceans of Cambrian time. Even the protoplasm that streams within each cell of our bodies has the chemical structure impressed on all living matter when the first simple creatures were brought forth in the ancient sea. And as life itself began in the sea, so each of us begins his individual life in a

miniature ocean within his mother's womb, and in the stages of his embryonic development repeats the steps by which his race evolved, from gill-breathing inhabitants of a water-world to creatures able to live on the land.

Rachel L. Carson, The Sea Around Us

It is not surprising that most primitive mythologies share a common character—the woman who lived in the sea. For the Eskimo, this procreator of life was Sedna.

## The Story of Sedna

Sedna was the offspring of two giants. From early childhood she was self-willed and stubborn. On reaching a marriageable age, she defied her father by refusing to wed any of the suitors he had in mind for her. Sedna loved a handsome young man, from a distant country, who had secretly courted her for a long time. Contrary to her father's wishes, she went to live with this young man amongst his own people, high on a rocky cliff overlooking the restless, wind-tossed waves. When she complained of hunger, the women brought her the food of a scavenger bird, which, in spite of her hunger, she could hardly swallow. Only then did she realize that her husband and his friends, althought they looked like people, were really fulmars.[9]

Although Sedna loved her husband, she was unaccustomed to the food and way of life of the

---

9. The fulmar is a bird of the petrel family. Like the sea gull, it is a scavenger living primarily on the refuse of the sea.

fulmar people. She longed for her old home. When her father visited them, wishing to be reconciled with his daughter and son-in-law, she complained bitterly to him of the food that the fulmars, the scavengers of the sea, provided for her. The father found that little persuasion was needed, on his part, to induce Sedna to return with him in his kayak.

As soon as he realized his wife had left him, the fulmar aroused his friends, who set out to scour the seas in search of the kayak. It was sighted, not far from shore, since the day was still too young for Sedna and her father to have put a great distance between themselves and their pursuers.

Swooping over the fugitives, the fulmars, with the beating of their wings, roused the sea to giant swells. Terrified, father and daughter beheld waves, mountain high, which lifted the fragile kayak skyward, where it poised for a moment motionless, then swept it downward, swirling in the clutch of the mighty waters.

Fearing for his own life, the father threw Sedna into the seething waters. In desperation, she clung to the kayak, only to have her father cut off her fingers, joint by joint, in his frantic struggle for survival. Then Sedna disappeared, swallowed into the depths of the ocean. However each joint of her fingers, as it fell into the sea, was transformed into a kind of sea life, such as seal, char, and beluga.

Thus Sedna became the goddess of the ocean, and the mother of all sea creatures. Since then, she has dwelt in the icy waters of the Arctic. The Eskimos say it is Sedna, when angry, who rouses the waters to gigantic waves that crash upon desolate shores. At such times, the shaman, or medicine man, journeys to her grotto. There he gently combs Sedna's hair to placate her anger since she, having no hands of her own, is unable to perform this task.

Thetis, the Sea-goddess, plays a significant role in Greek legends. At one time, Zeus himself sought her for a wife, but was informed by an oracle that the offspring of Thetis would be greater than the father. Therefore, fearing deposal in the same manner that he had seized power from *his* father, Cronus, Zeus judiciously bestowed Thetis on a hero named Peleus. Peleus had difficulty in winning the somewhat reluctant goddess, as she had the ability to change her shape. However, even though she transformed herself into fire, water, a lion, and a serpent, Peleus overcame her maidenly hesitation and won her. Achilles, son of Thetis and Peleus, and the hero of the Trojan Wars, was indeed a greater warrior than his father.

Thetis showed her power in many ways. She rescued Hephaestus, the god of the forge, when he was cast out of Mount Olympus because of his ungainly shape. In her grotto, she received Dionysus, the god of the vine and symbol of fertility, when he was pursued by Lycurgus after his army had been utterly destroyed. When she dipped her son, Achilles, in the River Styx, she made him invulnerable with the exception of his heel.

Later in Greek mythology, as the male played a more dominant role in what had hitherto been a matriarchal and matrilineal society, the goddesses assumed a secondary role. Poseidon, the earth-shaker, brother of Zeus and King of the Sea, was second only to Zeus himself. He resided in the depths of the sea where he kept his horses with brazen hoofs and golden manes. With these horses, he rode in a chariot over the waves of the sea, which were stilled at his approach.

To achieve success, the heroes of Greek legend

had to win the favour of the Sea-deity. Thus Jason was aided by Thetis and her Sea-nymphs, who saved the *Argo* and its crew from the perils of the Wandering Rocks. While Thetis with her hand on the rudder blade guided the ship on its course, the Sea-nymphs circled the vessel, raised it aloft on the billows they had created, and sent it away from the rocks where the water spouted and foamed.[10] Theseus, son of Poseidon, on his arrival at Crete, the kingdom of Minos, demonstrated his divine origin by retrieving, with the aid of the Nereids, the ring which Minos had cast into the sea as a challenge for the youthful hero.[11] Because he had incurred the enmity of Poseidon, the wily Odysseus was delayed ten years from returning to his kingdom in Ithaca after the Trojan Wars.

Early legends reflect not only man's awareness of the power of the sea (Oceanus) around him—a power that can shake the earth to its foundations—but also his awareness that the sea is the birthplace, the mother of all life.

In the artificial world of his cities and towns, man often forgets the true nature of his planet and the long vistas of history, in which the existence of the race of men has occupied a mere moment of time. The sense of all these things comes to him most clearly in the course of a long ocean voyage when he watches day after day the receding rim of the horizon, ridged and furrowed by waves; when at night he becomes aware of the earth's rotation as the stars pass overhead; or when alone in the world of water and sky, he feels the loneliness of his earth in space. And then, as never on

10. Apollonius, *Argonautica*, tr. Gilles. Cambridge University Press
11. Interesting accounts of the adventures of both Jason and Theseus are given in R.S. Lambert, *Myths, Legends and Fables*. The Book Society of Canada Limited

land, he knows the truth: that his world is a water
world, a planet dominated by its covering mantle of
ocean, in which the continents are but transient
intrusions of land above the surface of the
all-encircling sea.

> Rachel L. Carson, *The Sea Around Us*


Tyger! tyger! burning bright
In the forests of the night,
What immortal hand or eye
Could frame thy fearful symmetry?

> William Blake, "The Tyger"


Poets, philosophers, and indeed all thinking men
have long pondered the paradox of good and evil
existing in a world created and sustained by a benevolent creator. William Blake put the question
succinctly when, referring to the tiger, he asked, "Did
he who made the Lamb make thee?" Why do violence, brutality, a "nature red in tooth and claw"[12],
disease, plague, and death exist? Most religions and
legends are consistent in their approach to the
problem.

Evil was not present in the early phase of the
world's life, when man dwelt in a state of complete
bliss. Observe the similarities in the following
descriptions of this earthly paradise taken from the
*Bible*, Robert Graves's *The Greek Myths*, and Ella Elizabeth Clark's *Indian Legends of Canada*:


And the Lord God planted a garden eastward in Eden;
and there he put the man whom he had formed. And
out of the ground made the Lord God to grow every
tree that is pleasant to the sight, and good for food;


12. Alfred, Lord Tennyson, *In Memoriam*

the tree of life also in the midst of the garden, and the
tree of knowledge of good and evil.
And a river went out of Eden to water the garden. . . .

*Genesis II:8-10*


These men were the so-called golden race, subjects of
Cronus, who lived without cares or labour, eating only
acorns, wild fruit, and honey that dripped from the
trees, drinking the milk of sheep and goats, never
growing old, dancing and laughing much; death, to
them, was no more trouble than sleep. They are all
gone now, but their spirits survive as genii of happy
rustic retreats, givers of good fortune, and upholders
of justice.

Robert Graves, *The Greek Myths: I*


Long ago, all the peoples and the animals lived in
peace and happiness. There was no winter, with its
cold blasts and death-giving chill. There was always
food for everyone, for there were many deer in the
forests, herds of buffalo on the grassy plains, plenty of
fruit on bush and tree. Flowers bloomed everywhere.
The birds, dressed in more beautiful plumage than
today, filled the air with their songs. The beasts were
tame, and came and went at man's bidding. There was
no war. There was no fear of man, for no one would
harm another.

Ella Elizabeth Clark, *Indian Legends of Canada*


"They are all gone now"—the "golden race", and
the Golden Days. Trouble came, and according to
most accounts, it came in the guise of woman. The
following story of the creation of Evil bears certain
similarities to the account in the third chapter of
Genesis.

## Pandora's Box

In Greek legend, the immortal to whom mankind owes most gratitude is the Titan, Prometheus.[13] He it was who formed man from the dust of the earth; he it was whose solicitude, selflessness, courage, and endurance enabled his creation to survive, grow, and develop in wisdom. Prometheus was the only one of the immortals whose noble nature was not mixed with base matter.

Prometheus's brother, Epimetheus, whose name means "he who thinks afterwards", had created the animals. Bestowing on them warm coats with which to cover themselves, sharp claws and fangs with which to defend themselves, and fleetness of foot to escape their enemies, he left nothing for man, the last creation. However, to compensate for these advantages, Prometheus made man to stand upright so that he could contemplate the heavens, and gave him intelligence over the beasts of the forests. Since man had not been blest with the natural covering given to the animals Prometheus stole a piece of glowing ember from Mount Olympus, the home of the gods, and gave it to the race of men to protect them from the cold.

But Zeus was angry with Prometheus for he had already ordained that men should never enjoy the benefits of fire. When he looked down from Mount Olympus and beheld the flames, his rage knew no bounds. He realized that only Prometheus would have defied him in this manner, and he vowed to obtain vengeance by punishing mankind. He ordered Hephaestus, the god of the forge, to form a woman

13. See the story of Prometheus and creation in Jay Macpherson, *The Four Ages of Man*, Macmillan.

from clay. Each of the gods was asked to bestow a special gift upon her: thus Aphrodite gave her beauty; Athene, wisdom; Apollo, grace; and Hermes, subtlety. For this reason, she was named Pandora, which means "all gifted".

Adorned with beauty and graced with all the feminine attributes, Pandora was sent to visit Epimetheus. Before she left, Zeus handed her a great jar which he said was her dowry.

Realizing that Zeus would seek vengeance in some manner, Prometheus had warned Epimetheus never, under any circumstances, to open the jar.

Pandora and Epimetheus enjoyed a life of domestic felicity for several months until, as Zeus had planned, Pandora's curiosity got the better of her. As each day passed, her curiosity increased until it became so overwhelming a passion that she could resist no longer. With trembling fingers, she opened the jar, only to draw back in horror as its contents were revealed.

This jar had once belonged to Prometheus, who had packed away in it all the evils of the world. Now out of it poured monstrous shapes: cruel War, Famine with its pitiless leer, the grim, shroud-covered figure of Death, and the evil passions—Lust, Hatred, and Greed. Last, shot up a jet of stinking, noxious gas. In vain, the frantic girl attempted to replace the lid. Soon the gas, which consisted of Disease and Plague, enveloped the earth in a pestilent cloud. Then the jar was empty, except for one flying creature. This was Hope. Prometheus had kept it to console man. Thus, as long as the earth remains, Hope stays with us and mankind endures.

So great was Zeus's anger towards Prometheus for stealing fire that he sent two powerful servants to seize him and chain him to a rock in the Caucasian Mountains. Here he remained amidst driving rain, freezing gales, suffocating heat, and blazing sun. To add to these miseries, Zeus sent a huge vulture to tear away his liver. Since Prometheus was an immortal, he was not subject to death, but was forced to endure unspeakable agony forever.

Thus Zeus gained vengeance on Prometheus and thus the Golden Age of Mankind came to an end. No longer would man enjoy a leisurely life amidst a beneficent nature.

The story of Pandora has features common to many myths, the most salient of these being the two contrasting brothers. Prometheus, the benefactor of mankind, was wise, noble, and selfless; Epimetheus was stupid and selfish. These are the Cain and Abel counterparts of Greek mythology. In the Glooscap legends of the eastern coast of our country, Glooscap is Prometheus and his wicked wolf-brother, Malsumsis, is Epimetheus. Malsumsis was the creator of all that is harmful to man: rocks, thickets, and harmful animals. Glooscap formed the pleasant plains, the food plants, the helpful animals, and the human race.[14] In the Iroquois legends, Good Brother Glooscap made the harmful animals smaller and less fierce so that human beings would be able to master them.[15]

14. Cottie Burland, *North American Indian Mythology*
15. Ella Elizabeth Clark, *Indian Legends of Canada*

## Hermes and the First Barter

Sometimes, in both Greek and Indian legends, good and evil, instead of being depicted in two antagonistic figures, dwell within one person. Usually, as with Hermes, son of Zeus and Maia, and messenger of the gods, the evil is not malevolent, but mischievous. When he was one day old, Hermes stole Apollo's cattle. So wily was he that he had the cattle walk backwards away from a cliff in order to confuse his pursuers.

When Apollo learned the identity of the thief, he confronted Hermes with the crime. Hermes, wrapped in swaddling clothes, at first feigned innocence by pretending to sleep. Eventually he owned up, not only to the theft but also to the fact that he had already killed two of the cattle, and used the gut of one to make himself a lyre.

Hermes attempted to mollify the wrath of the aroused Apollo by playing a tune on his lyre and singing praises of the god. He then led Apollo to where the remainder of the cows were grazing and agreed to return these and give the newly invented lyre to Apollo in recompense for the two cows he had slain. Apollo readily agreed to this bargain.

Since this was the first barter ever made, Hermes has become the god of merchants. He is also the god of thieves. As to whether or not there is any connection between these two, let the reader be judge!

This mischievous figure appears in all Canadian Indian myth cycles: in Wesukechak of the Cree; Napi of the Blackfoot; Crow of the Kutchin; Raven, the creator-god among the Coast tribes of British Columbia; and Coyote, the mischief-maker in the legends of the western plateau tribes. The following story, which illustrates Coyote's dual role of benefactor of man and

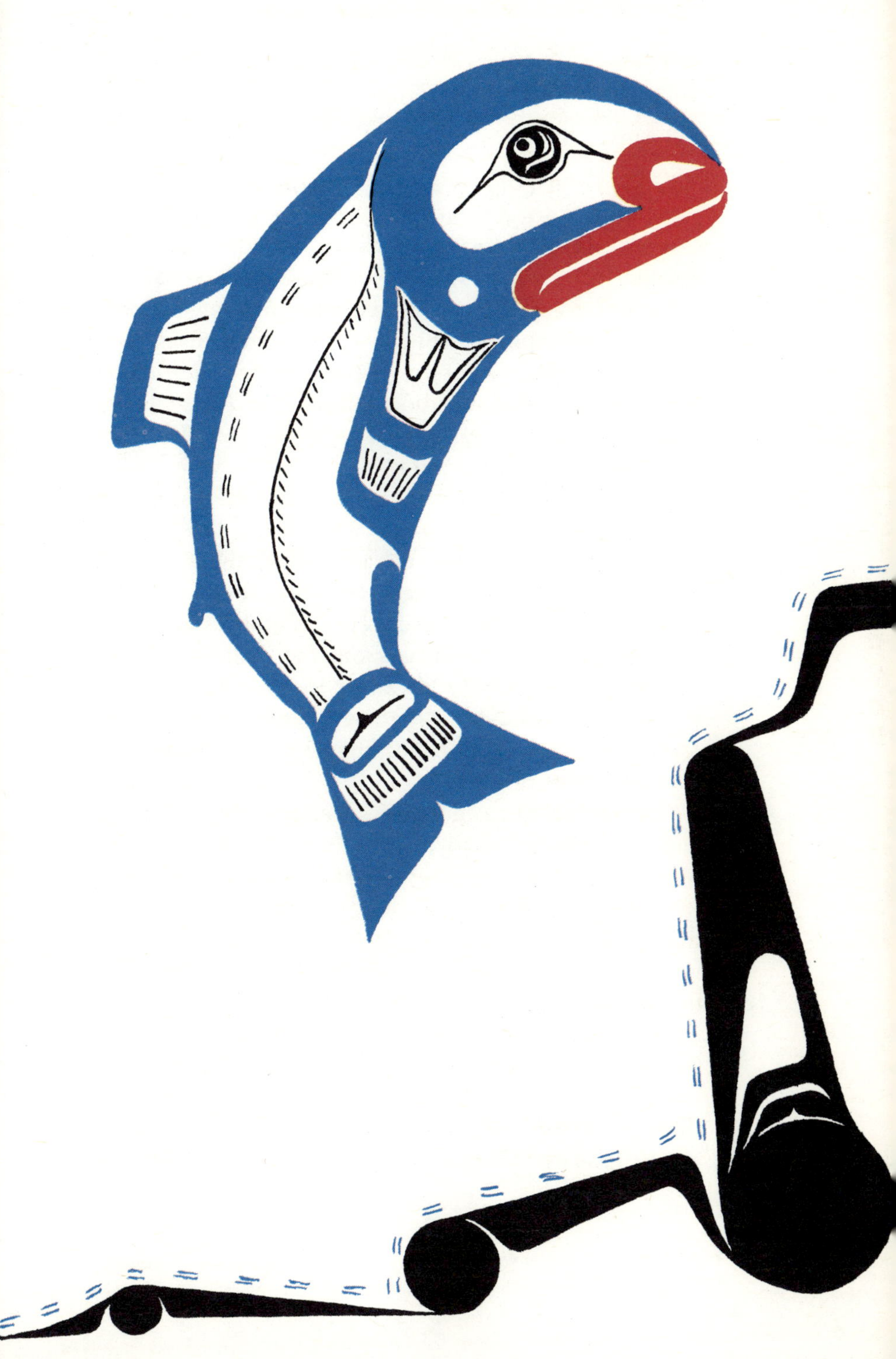

instigator of trouble, bears a striking resemblance to the story of Pandora.


## The Story of Coyote and the Salmon

Coyote, like Rabbit and Raven, had the ability to change his form at will. One day, while crossing a turbulent creek, he lost his balance and fell into the water. To escape drowning, he changed himself into a board and was swept downstream to the Thompson River. From it, he was borne down the Fraser River towards the sea. At last, he was stopped by a fish-dam owned by two old women.

The next day, the old women noticed the board and decided it would be just right for making a dish.

They placed salmon in this newly-fashioned dish, and sat down to dinner. Imagine their chagrin, however, when they discovered that the succulent salmon were disappearing from the dish so quickly that they could hardly get a bite to eat. The ravenous Coyote had discovered that he liked salmon too! At last, one of the women became angry and threw the dish into the fire.

Confronted once more with death, Coyote quickly changed himself into a baby wailing piteously in fright and pain. Quickly the frantic women plucked the baby from the fire, rubbed soothing ointment on his burns, and comforted him as well as they knew how to. "Let us," said one of the women, "bring up this baby as our own."

Time passed, and the child grew in stature, though he remained disobedient and fractious. One day the two women were going on a journey. Before leaving, they gave the young Coyote explicit instructions, keeping, as most parents do, the most important to the last. "Do not," they admonished, "under any circumstances, open any of the boxes which we must leave in your care."

Coyote promised, but being disobedient and headstrong, he had no intention of carrying out his promise. Besides, he had long been curious as to the contents of these boxes.

Now Coyote also had designs on the dam which had checked his progress to the sea. There were no salmon in Coyote's country, and he wanted his people, who lived farther upstream, to share the benefits of this delicious source of nourishment. Therefore the dam must be destroyed in order that the life-giving salmon might venture upstream to the waters of his people.

No sooner were the two old women out of sight than Coyote vigorously and remorselessly wrecked the dam. Then, both to defy the old women and to satisfy his curiosity, he proceeded to open the four forbidden boxes.

Out of the first box, poured forth jets of smoke; out of the second, hordes of angry wasps; from the third, clouds of blow-flies; and, from the fourth, an army of beetles.

As a result of Coyote's concern for his people, he was able to provide them with the salmon which he himself enjoyed so much. However, because he was disobedient, his people are tormented by smoke-wasps, salmon-flies, blow-flies, and meat-beetles, which every year reach their peak in the spring, at the time the salmon begin their run upstream.


## The Flood

The Book of the Rocks—i.e., the fossilized evidence of earth's early invertebrates—testifies that at one time the seas covered much of the earth's surface. Therefore it is not surprising that the religions of most early peoples contain accounts of floods. These accounts exhibit startling resemblances. The parallel between the following Greek story and the Biblical account of the Flood is obvious.

## *Philemon and Baucis*

After the creation of Pandora, the race of mankind multiplied and spread. Evil also increased; gross unnatural acts, selfishness, and violence sprang up everywhere like weeds in a garden, and sullied and obscured the flower of men's noble qualities. Zeus looked down from Mount Olympus in disgust at man, whom he had created. He decided to destroy man utterly.

First, he determined to see for himself if, in this morass of wickedness, any just man existed. Zeus, besides being king of the Gods, was also protector of travellers. Assuming the disguise of weary travellers, and trudging along the roads and byways of Phrygia, he and his son, Hermes, sought hospitality at the houses they chanced upon. But, even if a door were opened unto them, all they received was a contemptuous stare, a rude, heartless response to a request for food, or the slamming of the door in their faces. At each encounter, Zeus's mounting anger was reflected on his thunderous brow, and to Hermes he stormed, "Surely I am right to destroy man, for, in his selfishness, he has neglected his first duty: consideration to strangers."

Just as Zeus made this decision, they came to a humble dwelling somewhat removed from the roadway. Zeus hesitated; then turned and, followed by Hermes, climbed the path, which was almost hidden by ferns and wild flowers. Reaching the house, he knocked at the door.

Almost immediately, he heard the scraping of a bench along a rough floor and the shuffling of sandalled feet. Then the door creaked open to reveal a white-haired woman. On her wrinkled face were depicted both curiosity and concern. Beside her stood an old man, peering anxiously at the strangers. Quickly Zeus and Hermes explained their plight, and once more sought hospitality. Immediately, the faces of the old couple, whose names were Philemon and Baucis, relaxed in warm welcome. The old man opened the door wide. "We have not much to offer you," he piped, "but what we have is yours."

With as much alacrity as his years would allow, Philemon placed another bench beside the table at which he and his wife had been eating. Baucis, her hands trembling, placed a bowlful of steaming broth and a large chunk of newly baked bread before each of the guests. Then she cut two large pieces of cheese and filled a jug with wine. Placing this in the centre of the table, she bade the guests help themselves.

Then Baucis sat down beside her husband and readily responded to the questions asked by the disguised gods. Neither Philemon nor Baucis noticed that, although large draughts of wine had been consumed, the pitcher remained filled to the brim— until Hermes, after having poured from it for the third time, passed the still brimming pitcher to Zeus. Then Philemon realized that they were in the presence of gods. In terror, he and Baucis sank to their knees beseeching the immortals to have pity on them for offering such plain fare to the very gods themselves.

Zeus placed his hands on the shoulders of the trembling couple and said, "I shall destroy utterly those who have spurned me and rejected the opportunity to befriend strangers. But you, who have welcomed strangers without question, have shown that the race of man is worth preserving."

With that, he took them to a high hill overlooking the countryside. With a wave of his arm, a beautiful white palace appeared. Then Zeus uttered these words: "This is my temple and you, my loyal and tested servants, shall be the priests of this temple for as long as you shall live." With these words he and Hermes vanished as abruptly as the temple had appeared, while the old couple looked at each other in wide-eyed amazement.

After this, day after day, the rains came. The swollen, turbulent rivers overflowed their banks, and the valleys were flooded with water that destroyed everything in its wake. Then the sun broke through the lowering cloud. Its rays were reflected off the beautiful white palace that Zeus had built for Philemon and Baucis. In all that part of the country, this was the only building that had escaped the flood, and Philemon and Baucis were the only humans who remained alive.

For many years, they served in the temple the gods whom they had not neglected when they had appeared in human guise. Then, when the time came, as it must for all mortals, to enter into the realm of death, Philemon looked towards Baucis in amazement, for from her ears green shoots were sprouting. Baucis, in turn, saw that Philemon's limbs were being transformed into roots. "Farewell," they called to each other, "farewell", their voices fading away. Where they stood, a mighty oak puts forth its arms towards the sky; beside it, stands a slender linden, its branches intertwined with those of its taller companion. These are the only trees to be seen amidst the fens that encompass them.[16]

The Indian legends of the Flood differ somewhat from the Greek and Biblical accounts. Though most tribes had their own explanation, none give evidence of the Flood being a *punishment* for mankind. This was doubtless because Indian societies had not "developed" to the extent that the supreme spirit would feel the need to destroy mankind because of his evil, unnatural, or selfish acts. Most of the Indian accounts, for example those of the Dogrib, Slavey, and Iroquois, maintain a characteristic of primitive stories in having animals as the protagonists.

In one Indian legend, however, that of the Squamish tribe of British Columbia, the main characters are people. In addition, they are people who possess two of the noblest qualities which man can have: unselfishness and courage.

## The Squamish Account of the Flood

Long, long ago, in the mists of time, the heavens opened and the rains descended. Day after day, the

16. This is not the only Greek account of the Flood. Of similar nature is the story of Deucalion who, with his wife, Pyrrha, was spared by the intervention of Prometheus when Zeus decided to destroy mankind. This story, like the Biblical account of the Flood, contains an ark and a dove which Deucalion, like Noah, sent on an exploratory flight as the waters were subsiding. Mankind was renewed when Deucalion and Pyrrha cast rocks over their shoulders. These rocks became men or women, according to whether Deucalion or Pyrrha had thrown them. See Matthew III:9, "For I say unto you, that God is able of these stones to raise up children unto Abraham."

rain poured down; the mountain torrents cascaded in their ever-widening plunge to the valleys. Gradually, the rivers rose until they overflowed their brims and covered these valleys. The inland sea crept higher and higher, quietly taking possession of more and more land until the foothills were lost beneath its surface. And still the rains descended.

Seeking the only refuge in this world of water, the Indians retreated before the oncoming seas to the shores surrounding Lake Beautiful, in what is now British Columbia. Here, realizing that their whole nation faced a watery grave, they held a Great Council. At this council, they decided that a huge canoe should be built and a gigantic cable constructed to anchor it, so that the canoe would not be swept by the winds into the waters of the vast deep.

To the men fell the task of building this canoe. Goaded by the waters that drew closer and closer, they made no distinction between night and day in their efforts to finish the canoe. The women, aided by the light of pine torches at night, fashioned with cedar fibres the thickest and longest cable that had ever been made. With bleeding hands, they plaited the cable, chewing the fibres to make them more pliable, and oiling them to make them sea-resisting.

Realizing that their own lives were of little importance in relation to the renewal of the tribe itself, the people had chosen from their midst the bravest, strongest, handsomest youth and the most beautiful maiden. These two were to act as guardians for all the babies of the tribe, who were to be placed in the canoe. Fresh water and provisions were made ready for them. This was the only hope of survival now that the water threatened to submerge them at any moment.

As the waters crept closer and closer, strong hands

lifted the babies into the canoe. In the entire tribe, not a baby was overlooked; not a single person made an effort to save himself. Their only utterances were shouts of encouragement to the maiden who sat at the bow of the canoe to watch, and to the youth who knelt at the stern to guide. Just as the waters were about to stifle their voices forever, the courageous people cried their last farewells. They were seen and heard no more.

Still the rain poured down and the water rose. Then, after the canoe had been afloat for days and days, the rain ceased and the sun emerged, only to cast its rays on a world void of everything save an endless sea and a lone canoe which rode at anchor with its cargo.

Later, when the youth, keeping his watch, was peering ahead into the moon-glimmering waters, he discerned a peculiar shape. He was not certain what it was; he could only hope. Then, as day broke, he gave a shout of relief and joy. It was land—the top of a mountain.

As quickly as possible, he cut the cable which had secured the canoe to a huge boulder, now many leagues beneath the water's surface. Then with quick, strong strokes he paddled towards the mountain peak which seemed to be rising higher and higher out of the waters.

When they reached the mountain, which today is called Mount Baker, the waters had sunk sufficiently for the youth and maiden to place their precious cargo on its slopes. This done, they looked at the children who had been placed in their charge, then their hands clasped each other's.

The waters continued to retreat; soon the youth was able to build lodges to shelter the children, who each day grew stronger and taller. When they reached maturity, the world was repeopled by them.

As you look up at the peak of Mount Baker disappearing into the clouds, do not forget the sacrifice of these valiant, unselfish Squamish people who gave themselves that their children might live.

## The Worship of Physical Strength

As the legends of various races testify, early man venerated physical strength. Each has a legend of a Samson-like figure, possessing not only prodigious strength, but also a strong sense of duty or dedication to a noble cause.

Greek mythology has its mighty Heracles, famed for the twelve tasks he performed for King Eurystheus. Both Greek and Indian mythologies contain accounts of strong men who held up the sky. In Greek legend, Atlas strained for centuries under the mighty load of the sky. It was the Greek hero, Perseus, who put an end to Atlas's tormenting labours by holding before him the head of Medusa, the Gorgon. This head had the power to transform all who beheld it into stone. Now, where Atlas once bore the weight of the sky upon his shoulders, the lofty Atlas Mountains of North Africa disappear amongst the clouds. In Indian mythology, it was Aemaelk who sustained the weight of the heavens upon his shoulders.

## The Strong Man of the Tsimsyan Legends

"You are fit company for women and slaves. Yours will be the task to help the slaves when we return in our canoes loaded with sea lions."

Thus the three stalwart, handsome warriors taunted their younger brother, Aemaelk, who wasted his days in idleness, lingering amidst the ashes of the fire while the warriors devoted their energies to physical labours in preparation for the annual hunt for sea lions.

As everyone knows, the sea-lion hunt is a dangerous task demanding both physical strength and mental agility. For months and months, the lazy youth's brothers had been preparing themselves for the hunt, which would put to the test their manhood. Every morning at dawn, they would bathe in the icy waters of the ocean, an act of purification and of self-discipline undertaken before engaging in any difficult or dangerous mission. Then they would have their parents flay them with branches until the welts stood out on their bodies like weird tattoos. To increase the pain to almost unbearable agony, a brew consisting of huhlens roots was rubbed into the wounds. To develop their muscles, they went into the forests each day and broke off the branches of spruce trees. Every morning, the crashing of limbs, as huge branches were torn in two, could be heard in the village.

To all appearances, the lazy brother did nothing all this time. Unknown to the others, however, each night he would arise from the fireside, and go to the ocean and bathe. One evening, when a cold moon lighted the waters with magic, a loon emerged from the darkness of the outer waters and swam towards him. As it drew closer, its haunting voice cried out, "For many months I have seen you enduring the taunts of your wicked older brothers. Put your trust in me and I will give you strength. Take hold of my feet and have no fear, whatever befalls."

As the loon dived into the water, the youth followed and clutched its feet. Down, down they plunged through the moon-touched waters, until a mantle of darkness enshrouded them, and their feet touched the bottom of the sea. So unaccustomed were the youth's eyes to the lightless depths that he could scarcely discern the huge cavern that yawned before them.

Then the loon spoke again. "Walk to the far end of the cavern. There you will find a spring. Bathe in its waters and then return here. I shall be waiting for you."

The youth did as instructed, and, when he returned, found the loon at the mouth of the cave.

"After I have taken you back, continue to sit by the fire all day as if nothing had happened," instructed the loon.

Aemaelk did as the loon had told him. All day he lingered by the fire, disregarding the sneers and taunts of his brothers. At night, he secretly slipped into the forest and tested his strength by tearing off the branches of trees. His strength increased until he could bend full-grown pine trees like a bow.

The day of the seal hunt an air of eager expectancy hung over the village. The three older brothers had been assigned to the canoes of three of their uncles. When Aemaelk declared his intention of partaking in the sea-lion hunt, the uncles refused his offer. "Where were you when the others were training?" they asked. "Lazing by the fire amidst the dirt of the ashes. Stay with the women and slaves. There is no place for you here amongst the men."

Then his youngest uncle, feeling pity for the boy, turned to him and said, "There is always a place for you in my canoe whenever you want it. I am sure that there are many tasks that you can perform."

So he who was despised and rejected by all others found his place after all.

By the time they neared the island where the herds of sea lions gathered at this time of year, a strong wind had struck up from the north. From afar, the warriors heard the roar of the surf pounding on the rocky shore. On nearing the sea-lions' domain, they saw the waters eddying treacherously about the shoals that guarded the entrance, and beheld the breakers smiting the rocks amidst a shower of foam. The more fearful souls urged the leaders to return. But the uncles were resolute.

Just as the eldest uncle, balancing himself at the bow of his canoe, was preparing to leap to shore, the canoe struck a rock and was split in two. Amidst cries of terror, its occupants disappeared beneath the turbulent sea. Then the next uncle courageously leaped from the bow of *his* canoe. He succeeded in landing on the rock, but his foot slipped on its treacherous surface and he fell. He was attacked by the sea lions, who tore his body asunder.

Then Aemaelk shouted to his uncle, "I shall leap ashore and kill the sea lions. You guide the canoe."

In vain, his uncle and the other warriors tried to dissuade him. "How can you hope to succeed," they cried, "when others who are stronger and better prepared have failed?" But Aemaelk held to his purpose and his uncle reluctantly let him take what he believed would be his deathleap.

Aemaelk stood up on the bow of the canoe. Though it pitched violently in the angry sea, he kept his balance as if rooted to the spot. Then, as the canoe was borne aloft on the crest of a giant wave, he sprang for the shore. Just as he landed, a sea lion bore down upon him. Quickly, Aemaelk sprang to his feet, seized the sea lion by the throat and threw it over on its back, killing it instantly. In like manner, he disposed of many others. Whenever the canoe was borne up on the crest of a wave, he tossed the bodies aboard. When the craft was filled, he jumped aboard and they returned to the village.

This was the first of many feats of strength and courage that Aemaelk performed. Later, when the wrestlers of his tribe had been shamefully beaten by a giant of the Wudsae tribe, he redeemed the honour of the Tsimsyans by defeating this giant with ease. Similarly, he bested the warriors of all other tribes in feats of strength until his fame spread throughout the land, and people realized that his strength was more than mortal. Aemaelk's greatest task, however, was yet to be performed.

One night, while he was sleeping by the fireside, as was still his custom, a long canoe approached. Silently, it touched the shore. One occupant quietly sprang out and, without a word, strode directly to where the youth was sleeping. Touching him gently on the shoulder, he said, "Your grandfather is growing old and weary and needs you."

As though he had been expecting this, Aemaelk rose immediately to his feet and followed the stranger to the beach, where he took the place that had been prepared for him near the bow of the canoe. Not a word was said to break the stillness of the night. Without a paddle being raised, the canoe glided out to sea. Silently, it moved westward in the path the sun takes before disappearing from view, passed the last of the offshore islands and, long after, came to a lonely island, bleak and desolate, its flat surface barely higher than the level of the sea. Here Aemaelk and the stranger prepared to land.

As soon as the canoe touched this strange shore, all the crew, except the man who had spoken to Aemaelk,

were transformed into loons. With the command, "Follow me," the man led Aemaelk inland until they came to an opening in the ground so deep that Aemaelk could not see to the bottom. With a motion of his arm, the stranger indicated that Aemaelk was to follow him down a ladder that disappeared into the depths of the earth.

After what seemed hours, Aemaelk and his guide reached the bottom. Here was a wooden platform and an ancient man straining under the weight of a huge hemlock pole.

"This man is your grandfather," said the stranger. "Since the world began he has held up the sky so that it would not fall upon the earth. Now he is old and tired, and has asked that you take his place. We know that you are fully prepared to do so."

Without hesitation, Aemaelk clasped his strong hands around the huge pole. Slowly the old man rose to his feet, gradually transferring the huge weight to Aemaelk. Then he said, "Be careful that you do not move, for every time you shift your weight, violent earthquakes will occur. If you allow the pole to slip, the heavens will fall and the earth be completely destroyed. These loons will be your messengers. They will supply your needs, such as food and water. Now I go to my rest, confident that you can carry on my task."

To this day, Aemaelk, who once dwelt amongst the Tsimsyan people, sustains the world by keeping the weight of the skies upon his shoulders.


These are the stories of long ago when the hills told the glory of creation, the stars sang together, and the heavens rejoiced. Today, many people feel that the cold, factual, scientific explanation of the earth's origin and history has deprived us of the wonder that accompanied the creation stories. For others, the wonder, the majesty, and the mystery surrounding creation and the development of life on this planet are as evident in the scientific explanation as in the mythical accounts.

> It is interesting to contemplate a tangled bank, clothed with many plants of many kinds, with birds singing on the bushes, with various insects flitting about, and with worms crawling through the damp earth, and to reflect that these elaborately constructed forms, so different from each other, and dependent upon each other in so complex a manner, have all been produced by laws acting around us. These laws, taken in the largest sense, being Growth with Reproduction; Inheritance which is almost implied by reproduction; Variability from the indirect and direct action of the conditions of life, and from use and disuse: a Ratio of Increase so high as to lead to a Struggle for Life, and as a consequence to Natural Selection, entailing Divergence of Character and Extinction of less-improved forms. Thus, from the war of nature, from famine and death, the most exalted object which we are capable of conceiving, namely, the production of the higher animals, directly follows. There is a grandeur in this view of life, with its several powers, having been originally breathed by the Creator into a few forms or into one; and that, whilst this planet has gone cycling on according to the fixed law of gravity, from so simple a beginning endless forms most beautiful and most wonderful have been and are being evolved.
>
> Charles Darwin, *Origin of Species*

# 2
# Love

Greater love has no man than this, that he lay down
his life for his friends.

John XV:13

Literature bears testimony to the responsive chord
which this sentiment strikes in the heart of man.
Ruth's selfless devotion to Naomi, "Whither thou
goest, I will go; and where thou lodgest, I will lodge:
thy people shall be my people, and thy God my God:
where thou diest, will I die, and there will I be buried
. . . "[1] is perhaps the most eloquent recorded witness
of devotion of one human for another.

Pyramus and Thisbe, Orpheus and Eurydice,
Alcyone and Ceyx, and Hero and Leander are but a
few examples from Greek mythology of selfless
devotion and sacrifice for love.[2]

The Indians, who understood the concepts of

unselfishness, devotion, and fidelity, narrated many stories involving a beautiful maiden, a handsome youth, and often the tragic death of one or both. The ancient Greeks conceived of rivers as the playgrounds of nymphs and water-spirits. Similarly, from the east coast of our country to the Pacific, the Indians associated a beautiful or striking scene with a story of true love. Thus Heart Lake, now part of a provincial park near Brampton, was (in legend) formed when an Indian princess wept for her lover who had been killed in battle. As she wept, the tears dropping at her feet formed a pool which grew wider and wider, until it assumed the shape of her heart, now broken for love. The beautiful Lake of the Mountains, near Picton, is an appropriate backdrop for the story of the lovely Mohawk princess, Tayouroughay, whose fidelity to her lover, the noble Gowanda, triumphed over parental opposition and the foisting on her of an unwelcome suitor. Entwined in the waters of the Tulameen, in British Columbia, is the spirit of an Indian maiden who died by its banks to save her true love. In the plunging of the river down its canyon, the sobbing of her farewells to her beloved can still be heard.

The echo in the valley through which the Qu'Appelle River flows awakened the imaginations of the Crees. All the stories involve true love, and are based on the name of the river, (in French, "Qu'Appelle"; in Cree, "Katapaywie sepe"; in English, "Who Calls"). None, however, is more

1. Ruth I: 16, 17

2. See the stories of Pyramus and Thisbe and Hero and Leander in Thomas Bulfinch, *The Age of Fable*, Airmont Paperbacks. The story of Orpheus and Eurydice is narrated on page 74 of this book; that of Alcyone and Ceyx on page 163.

beautifully narrated than "The Pilot of the Plains"
which, though written by a Mohawk, was inspired by
the Cree legends.

## The Pilot of the Plains

"False," they said, "thy Pale-face lover, from the land
    of waking morn;
Rise and wed thy Redskin wooer, nobler warrior
    ne'er was born;
Cease thy watching, cease thy dreaming,
    Show the white thine Indian scorn."

Thus they taunted her, declaring, "He remembers
    naught of thee:
Likely some white maid he wooeth, far beyond the
    inland sea."
But she answered ever kindly,
    "He will come again to me."

Till the dusk of Indian summer crept athwart the
    western skies;
But a deeper dusk was burning in her dark and
    dreaming eyes,
As she scanned the rolling prairie,
    Where the foothills fall and rise.

Till the autumn came and vanished, till the season of
    the rains,
Till the western world lay fettered in midwinter's
    crystal chains,
Still she listened for his coming,
    Still she watched the distant plains.

Then a night with nor'land tempest, nor'land snows
    a-swirling fast,
Out upon the pathless prairie came the Pale-face
    through the blast,

Calling, calling, "Yakonwita,
  I am coming, love, at last."

Hovered night above, about him, dark its wings and
  cold and dread;
Never unto trail or tepee were his straying footsteps
  led;
Till benumbed, he sank, and pillowed
  On the drifting snows his head,


Saying, "O my Yakonwita, call me, call me, be my
  guide
To the lodge beyond the prairie—for I vowed ere
  winter died
I would come again, beloved;
  I would claim my Indian bride!"

"Yakonwita, Yakonwita," O the dreariness that
  strains
Through the voice that calling, quivers, till a whisper
  but remains!
"Yakonwita, Yakonwita,
  I am lost upon the plains!"

But the Silent Spirit hushed him, lulled him as he
  cried anew,
"Save me, save me, O beloved, I am Pale, but I am
  true!
Yakonwita, Yakonwita,
  I am dying, love, for you!"

Leagues afar, across the prairie, she had risen from her
  bed,
Roused her kinsmen from their slumber: "He has
  come to-night,"
    she said
"I can hear him calling, calling,
  But his voice is as the dead.

"Listen!" and they sat all silent, while the tempest
  louder grew,

And a spirit-voice called faintly, "I am dying, love, for
  you."
Then they wailed, "O Yakonwita,
  He was Pale, but he was true!"

Wrapped she then her ermine round her, stepped
  without the tepee door,
Saying, "I must follow, follow, though he call for
  evermore,
'Yakonwita, Yakonwita,'"
  And they never saw her more.

Late at night, say Indian hunters, when the starlight
  clouds or wanes,
Far away they see a maiden, misty as the autumn
  rains,
Guiding with her lamp of moonlight
  Hunters lost upon the plains.

E. Pauline Johnson

## The River of Whispering Ghosts

### A Legend of the Western Prairies

Not far to the west of Calgary, almost in the shadow
of the Rocky Mountains, runs the River of
Whispering Ghosts. It's not a big stream, but it has a
history that will stick in your mind long after the
memory of the river itself has faded.

The story runs like this. In the old days, before the
white man came, there were two tribes of Indians in
this district, the Sarcees and the Blackfoot. They are
firm friends and allies now, but this was many years
ago and they fought each other bitterly for the right to
hunt elk in the foothills and buffalo on the prairies.
They had been at war for generations and the chiefs
of both tribes knew that it was time to stop all this and
come to an agreement before more of the best

warriors were killed off. There seemed no way to peace without a loss of dignity on one side or the other.

One summer, the chief of the Sarcees gave a great feast to which he invited everybody from far around, including the chief of the Blackfoot people, enemies though they were. The feast was to give the Sarcee chief an opportunity of announcing that his only boy child, Lipoto, was to become his "favorite son", which meant that every possible right, privilege, and honor would be heaped on him from then on.

The chief of the Blackfoot people was puzzled. This was something new indeed! An invitation to a feast, and from the chief of the Sarcees, who had been on the war path against the Blackfoot for so long. What was he to do?

He determined to call all the older men in council—men who were famous for their war deeds, the many horses they had stolen, the many coups they had counted, and the scalps they had brought home for the women to dance and sing around in the scalp dance.

For a long time they debated, the old men speaking loudly and insistently, the younger ones sitting quietly by and listening. Was this just a trap? It was an old familiar scheme, to invite people to a feast and then give them so much to eat and drink that they grew careless. Then, what was easier than to kill them as they slept?

But then, there was the boy, Lipoto. Surely they would never plan such a thing right after an important ceremony, nor would they risk a fight in which Lipoto might be killed. No, it was better to accept the invitation in the hope that it might be the beginning of a better understanding and lead to peace.

So the Blackfoot chief attended the feast and brought with him his wife and his only daughter, Winona, a beautiful and accomplished girl of sixteen.

Naturally, the two young people fell deeply and incurably in love with each other or there would be no legend about them.

They had little or no chance of speaking to each other and, while the ceremonies were still going on, there were so many people about that it was quite impossible to arrange a secret meeting.

When all was over, the Blackfoot chief moved his camp to the far side of the river and stayed there overnight. This was the chance that Lipoto had been waiting for. On the pretext of taking his horse to drink, he rode down to the ford to where he could see Winona when she came down to the river to get water for her mother.

In the sign language, known to all prairie Indians, Lipoto signalled that he would meet her on the river bank shortly after moonrise, and to this she agreed.

That night, when all were asleep, Lipoto stole down to the river. Was that Winona he could dimly see on the other side of the swift water?

"Winona?" he whispered, as loudly as he dared. He could hear no answer, though she had heard him and called softly back, "Lipoto!"

The noise of the wind in the willows and the lapping of the water prevented him from hearing her answer and so, feeling certain that each was waiting on the other side of the stream, they both advanced into the black and icy waters.

"Winona?"

"Lipoto?"

Each sought the other desperately, struggling, looking, calling, at each moment more distraught, till both were swept away and never heard of again.

Even today, if you go down to the River of Whispering Ghosts, you may hear them, still whispering for fear that they may be heard, pleading, sobbing. Or is it only the wind in the willows calling "Winona", and the lapping of the waves that answers softly, "Lipoto"?

Dr. Douglas Leechman

## The Legend of the Wishing Well

"What want we? Have we not perpetual streams,
Warm woods, and sunny hills, and fresh green
fields?"

William Wordsworth, *"The Recluse"*

"The Legend of the Wishing Well" has for its setting the countryside of southern Ontario.

If you turn from the highway leading west from London and climb a slope that rises from the banks of the Thames River, you will see a rivulet twisting and turning amidst the rocks. If you make a wish as you drink from the crystal clear waters of this stream, your wish will come true. This waterfall is known to the white man as the Wishing Well. It is the source of a legend[3] about another Indian maiden called Winona.

This Winona was the daughter of the chief of the Munsees, a tribe that called this region home long before the coming of the white man. Because of her beauty and position—the Munsees were a rich and powerful tribe—young braves came from afar seeking her hand in marriage. Of all her suitors, she looked with favour on two, only—Wignoed and Magana, both handsome young braves of the Delaware tribe.

Her father favoured Wignoed, for he was the more successful hunter and would be better able to provide for Winona. Magana was the faster runner and more

3. Of a similar nature is the Attiwondoron legend of the beautiful Naskwooksie. Following the death of her lover, Aromocho, who was killed by the Iroquois, Naskwooksie died and was turned into a spring now called Aromocho Springs. This is near Elmira, Ont. An Indian song describes the spring, "Clear as the character of the beautiful Naskwooksie, pure as the love of the twain."

skilful wrestler. Although he excelled at the various sports in which the warriors engaged, he was too sensitive to be a good hunter. Often he let a deer escape because he was enthralled by its graceful form and movement. Wignoed taunted him for this "softness", but Magana's kindness won him favour with Winona.

Each Indian brave vied with the other in contests of strength and skill to win the hand of this beautiful maiden. The results were always the same. Wignoed was the more successful hunter, but Magana triumphed at the sports. Knowing the wishes of her father, yet yearning to answer the dictates of her own heart, Winona was unwilling to acknowledge either as the winner and declared that they were equal and that all strife should cease between them.

Yet, as the days passed, the rivalry between the two warriors increased. Wignoed, in particular, resented Winona's indecision. Was he not the greater hunter and the wealthier of the two? His bitterness increased as, day by day, he saw too evident indications that Winona favoured Magana.

One evening, as the sun retreated beyond the forest cover of oak and maple, two figures could be seen, hand in hand, ascending the slope above the encampment. Their movements were light and carefree, like the little winds that play over the waving grasses. The two figures were Winona and Magana, and each was aware of the love that dwelt within the heart of the other.

Unbeknown to them, however, a third figure had slipped stealthily from the shelter of the camp, and, under cover of twilight and obscured by tree trunks, was pursuing them. The rapid beating of his heart and the baleful look he cast at the lovers betokened the

jealousy that filled his heart. This third figure was Wignoed.

Reaching the crest of the hill, Magana turned and whispered to Winona. Then the two figures standing at the brow of the hill silhouetted against the grey evening sky became one as Magana held Winona in his arms.

Suddenly, the snapping of a branch betrayed the presence of Wignoed. He burst from his cover, his face twisted and ugly under its evil mask of rage. An object hurtled through the air. This was followed by a sickening thud. With a cry, Magana sank to the ground, his breast pierced by the tomahawk of Wignoed.

With the frenzied strength of a dying man, Magana plucked the weapon from his breast, hurled it at Wignoed and thereby felled him.

Winona's screams quickly summoned her tribesmen. When they reached the hilltop, they beheld Magana and Wignoed, side by side in death. Their hands, which in life had been raised against one another, now touched in death. Their faces expressed peace and contentment, as though they had entered the Happy Land of the Hereafter.

Winona had disappeared. Where she had been standing, a stream of clear water burst from the ground. From the crest of the hill, the water tumbled and leapt joyfully amongst the rocks till it joined the river flowing serenely below.

The Indians call this stream the "Holy Spout", for those who wash in its waters purify themselves, and are certain to follow Winona, who has gone before them to the Land of the Hereafter where peace and goodwill dwell perpetually.

Whoever stands by this stream as it plunges down

the rocks, can hear, if he listens intently, the voice of Winona calling, "Magana, Magana, my beloved".

## Love Among the Stars

According to Greek legend, the Titan Prometheus created man so that he could stand upright. Thus man was different from the animals: he could look upwards to the heavens, the eternal realm; whereas the vision of the animals was restricted to the earth, the dust from which they were created and to which they would return. Throughout man's comparatively brief span on this planet, he has lifted his eyes onto the heavens and seen the glory of God. He has sought a link with the eternal realm as represented by the heavenly bodies.

The poet Binyon, to convey the thought that those who die for their country shall be remembered by posterity, wrote:

> As the stars that shall be bright when we are dust
> Moving in marches on the heavenly plain;
> As the stars that are starry in the time of our darkness
> To the end, to the end they remain.

Wordsworth wrote of the poet Milton:

> Thy soul was like a Star and dwelt apart,
> Pure as the naked heavens, majestic, free.

John Magee, aviator-poet, sensed a contact with the divinity:

> And, while with silent, lifting mind I've trod
> The high, untrespassed sanctity of space,
> Put out my hand and touched the face of God.

It was this sense of awe that, in 1968, prompted William Anders, James Lovell, and Frank Borman, the conquerors of space, to read, in turn, from the first chapter of Genesis when they viewed the surface of the moon a scant seventy miles' distance from their spaceship.

In all religions, the heavenly bodies play a significant role. Heavenly life is represented as a perfect concept of its counterpart on earth. In some primitive religions, humans were sacrificed to propitiate the sun, the King of the Heavens.

From early stages of man's history to modern times, astrologers have affirmed that the stars govern our lives. As a natural consequence of this almost universal worship of the astral bodies, Love, the supreme emotion of mankind, is associated with the stars.

In the Christian religion, the star of Bethlehem was a harbinger announcing the love of God for man. In Greek stories, the moon-goddess Selene was in love with a handsome mortal named Endymion. When she saw him asleep in a cave in Mount Latmus, she bent down and kissed his closed eyes. Endymion then fell into a dreamless sleep from which he has not yet wakened. He has never grown older. He preserves the glow of youth on his handsome face; his sleeping lids, forever closed, are still caressed by the moon maid as she looks down on him from her heavenly abode.

The constellations, Perseus and Andromeda, immortalize two lovers famed in Greek story.[4] Perseus had first discovered Andromeda chained to a rock. Here she was being sacrificed to a sea-monster who was ravaging her father's kingdom and who

4. Read the story of Perseus and Andromeda, R.S. Lambert, *Myths, Legends and Fables.*

could be placated only by the sacrifice of the beautiful Andromeda. Perseus changed the monster to a rock by showing it the Gorgon's head which he was carrying, and in this way rescued Andromeda, whom he later married.

The Indians, too, have their stories of love associated with celestial figures.

## The North Star

During the warm summer months Feather Woman and her sister used to sleep in the long grasses outside the family lodge. One morning, Feather Woman awoke earlier than usual. Morning Star, the last star to linger in the heavens as the Sun Chief approached, still looked down upon the earth, as if reluctant to depart. As Feather Woman gazed upward, the star seemed to shine more and more brightly, until a radiant light which glowed round it assumed the form of an Indian brave. His countenance was illuminated in lustrous beauty. To her companion, Feather Woman said, "O Tokana, I have fallen in love with Morning Star. He is by far the handsomest warrior I have ever seen."

Summer made way for autumn, when the leaves put on their gaudy colours and the birds made ready for their flight from approaching winter's cold breath. Early one morning, as Feather Woman was returning from the river, where she had gone to fetch water, a tall brave stood on the pathway blocking her way. Being timid and shy, Feather Woman hesitated before coming nearer to the stranger. He was proud of bearing, with bronze skin which glowed in the morning sunlight, and eyes which looked down on her kindly.

As if to allay her fears, he spoke. "O beautiful maiden of the Blackfoot, never in all my journeys above the earth had I gazed on such beauty as yours when I beheld you many moons ago, sleeping in the tall grasses outside your home. I aroused the anger of my father, Sky Chief, by forgetting to take my departure at the accustomed time. Know that I am Morning Star and that I am come to ask you to accompany me to the home of my father in the sky. Will you come, Feather Woman?"

Feather Woman's heart answered, "Yes, yes," but to her surprise she heard a voice which she scarce realized was her own replying, "First I must go to the lodge of my father to ask his permission."

"No," replied Morning Star, "if you love me truly, you will tell no one, but will come with me now to the land of my father."

Hesitantly, Feather Woman agreed. Although she loved Morning Star, it grieved her to leave forever her mother and father and the happy scenes of her childhood.

Morning Star took her by the hand and led her to a spider web, so large that it disappeared into the sky. He told her to hold tightly to the strands and close her eyes.

Feather Woman did so, and soon she found herself in a land much like the hills and forests of her homeland except that the fields and streams were bathed in a far more radiant light. Morning Star again took her by the hand and led her to a huge lodge that stood in a clearing in the forests. Here dwelt the Moon, mother of Morning Star. Morning Star bade Feather Woman enter. Inside, he addressed his mother:

"Mother, this is Feather Woman, she of whom I spoke to you several moons ago when I first looked down upon her beauty. Now she shall be my wife and your daughter."

The Moon welcomed Feather Woman to her new home in the skies. When Sky Chief returned at evening from his journey around the earth, he too was kind and gracious in his welcome.

The months that followed were happy ones. Feather Woman was with Morning Star, whom she loved, and with the Sun and the Moon, who looked on her as their daughter. Her former home in the world below seemed remote. Her thoughts seldom dwelt on her own father and mother. When a son, whom they named Star Boy, was born unto her, her happiness was complete.

Soon after the birth of Star Boy, the Moon gave Feather Woman a root digger, accompanying the gift with these words, "With this root digger you may dig all kinds of roots except the huge turnip that grows near the home of Spider Man. If you dig this root, unhappiness is certain to follow."

Feather Woman promised. But as day followed day, like Pandora, overwhelming curiosity overcame her. What would happen if she dug up the turnip? Day after day, she subdued this ever-increasing temptation to disobey the Moon's instructions, but the time came when her curiosity was too strong to resist.

One morning, in the absence of Sky Chief, after she had been digging the roots permitted to her, she edged closer and closer to the huge turnip. Looking about her and seeing no one, she hurriedly began to dig and pry. The immense turnip did not budge. Then she dug a trench around its root, thrust the root digger under it as far as it would go and strained at it with all her strength. The turnip stirred, but almost immediately shifted back into place. Feather Woman dug and heaved at the root all through the morning until, just as she was on the point of giving up, the turnip yielded. With her ebbing strength, she was able to pry it from its position.

To her amazement, a hole in the sky gaped at her. This was the entrance to the sky through which she had entered long ago! Cautiously she approached the edge and looked down. Far, far below she beheld the earth, its lakes and rivers like a beaded necklace threading through clumps of forest. An immense loneliness overwhelmed her. The picture of her father's lodge, her mother tanning hides, and her sisters returning from the hills after gathering berries was as vivid as if she were down on earth amongst them. Then she looked around at the bright sky land that surrounded her.  Feather Woman wept.

Sorrowfully, she returned to the lodge of the Moon and Sky Chief. As soon as the Moon saw her tear-stained face, she knew what had happened.

Sadly she spoke. "You have disobeyed us. Now you must return to your home on earth. Since you have seen the hills and streams of your homeland, your heart will be there and you can never be happy with us."

Feather Woman pleaded to be allowed to stay, for she loved Morning Star. But when Sky Chief returned and heard what had happened, neither her tears nor her entreaties prevailed. Back to the world whence she had come, Feather Woman and her child, Star Boy, were condemned to go.

After their return, Feather Woman and her son dwelt some five years on earth. Though her heart was gladdened by the warmth with which her parents welcomed her, true happiness was never hers again; on earth, she felt herself an exile from sky land and the husband she loved.

The hole in the sky through which Feather Woman

was drawn up into the bright land, and through which she was lowered again to earth, permits the radiant light of Sky Chief to shine down on us at night. It is called the North Star. Amidst all the moving stars of the heavens, it alone remains constant and unchanging.

## The Story of the Woman in the Moon

This story concerns the Ojibway,[5] an Indian tribe that roamed the forests of the Big Water, now called Lake Superior. Unlike Selene, Goddess of the Moon, who fell in love with Endymion, a shepherd, in this legend Lone Bird, a mortal, falls in love with the Moon.

Lone Bird, the only child of her father, Dawn of Day, had been endowed by Manitou with many graces: her movements were as light as the birch that sways in the breeze; her voice, melodious as the murmuring waters of the Kaministiquia; her face, unmatched in beauty by that of any other maiden of the tribe. Soon young braves from all parts of the country surrounding the inland sea came to Dawn of Day seeking his daugher's hand in marriage.

One gift, however, had been denied Lone Bird: the gift of love. Try as he might, her father could not persuade her to accept any of the handsome lovers.[6]

5. Ojibway or Ojibwa in Ontario; Chippewa in the United States; Saulteaux in Manitoba.
6. The Ojibway story resembles the Greek myth "Atalanta's Race". In each story, the maiden is scornful of men. Atalanta, the votary of Artemis, had sworn an oath of chastity. Lone Bird remained aloof from mortal men. Both stories are associated with the moon, which, because of its whiteness, symbolized purity. Both stories involve contests. See Edith Hamilton, "Atalanta", *Mythology*, Mentor Books.

To all their entreaties, her heart remained cold as the ice-locked water of the northern lakes.

At the end of his patience, Dawn of Day resolved that the matter of choosing a husband for Lone Bird could be put off no longer. Summoning the elders of the tribe, he asked them to make it known that a contest of skill and strength would be held amongst the young men of the tribe. To the winner, would be given the most cherished gift that he possessed, his daughter Lone Bird. On his return to his lodge, her father told Lone Bird to be prepared to take herself a husband.

When the day of the contest drew near, the flower, not only of the Ojibway youth, but of neighbouring tribes as well, gathered in the village. Each warrior, bent on one purpose—to win the contest and the hand of Lone Bird—was indifferent to the admiring glances cast on him by other dark-eyed beauties of the tribe. Significantly, in all the village, only one maiden was missing from the scene of the contest—Lone Bird. She sat apart in the lodge of her father, weeping.

The warriors vied with one another, each determined that he alone would prove himself worthy of the hand of Lone Bird. By midday, however, the contest had been narrowed to two warriors, Bending Bow and Who-Strikes-the-Game. Each far surpassed the other warriors in strength, skill, and fleetness of foot. Yet strive as they might, neither could triumph over the other. Races were run three times in an endeavour to break the deadlock between the two. In the hunting contests, each returned with exactly the same number of animal skins. In wrestling, though the bout continued long into the night, neither succeeded in pinning the other.

The heart of Dawn of Day was sorely troubled, for he looked on this deadlock as an ill omen.

When he returned to his lodge, Lone Bird threw herself at his feet. "O Father!" she cried. "Why do you wish to rid yourself of me? Do you begrudge the food and the skins used for me? Are you and She Eagle, my mother, entirely indifferent to the love I bear you that you wish to cast me from you like a dog that is no longer useful?"

The heart of Dawn of Day was touched. Now he realized the significance of the omen: no one was to possess Lone Bird; henceforth, she was destined to dwell in the lodge of her father and mother.

The years passed. As the sun's glow gives place to the soft hues of twilight, so the radiance of Lone Bird's youth yielded to a tranquil beauty.

One day, as she was returning from the stream with water, she paused, sat on a flat rock, and looked around. For the first time in her life, an immense loneliness welled up within her. She looked at the birds fluttering in pairs from shrub to shrub, at the flowers growing in twos from the branch. Everything in nature seemed to join with something else. The waters of the stream mingled with the inland sea; the earth yielded before the touch of the sun's rays. She alone, she who had rejected all her suitors, was unmated to another being. The day would come when her father and mother would depart for the Land of Shadows and she would indeed be alone.

For the remainder of the day she sat, overwhelmed with her melancholy thoughts. Then evening drained the brightness from the landscape. The halftones of twilight matched her mood. The Moon began his circuit of the heavens, his white light rippling over the water of the lake.

Lone Bird looked up to the Moon, whose serene beauty lent a magic to everything he touched, and her heart went out to him as it never had to any mortal suitor. She sighed, "You are handsomer by far than Bending Bow or Who-Strikes-the-Game. Would that I could leave this world and dwell with you forever."

The Good Spirit heard her and carried her to the heavens placing her gently into the arms of the Moon.

Lone Bird, the Woman in the Moon, has dwelt in the arms of the Moon ever since, having found in heaven a happiness that she never knew on earth.

## The World Beyond Death

How do I love thee? Let me count the ways.
I love thee to the depth and breadth and height
My soul can reach when feeling out of sight
For the ends of Being and ideal Grace.
I love thee to the level of everyday's
Most quiet need, by sun and candlelight.
I love thee freely, as men strive for Right;
I love thee purely, as they turn from Praise.
I love thee with the passion put to use
In my old griefs, and with my childhood's faith.
I love thee with a love I seemed to lose
With my lost saints,—I love thee with the breath,
Smiles, tears, of all my life!—and, if God choose,
I shall but love thee better after death.

Elizabeth Barrett Browning, Sonnets from the Portuguese

The above sonnet affirms the Christian faith: the grave is not the end, but the beginning of a new life—a life where we are reunited in spiritual form with loved ones who have gone before us.

Some, however, lacking Elizabeth Barrett Browning's Christian optimism, have been reluctant to wait for death to establish this nebulous reunion, and have tried themselves to bridge the chasm separating the living from the dead. A former prime minister of Canada attempted through the medium of spiritualism to communicate with his mother, to whom he had been devoted in life. Sir Arthur Conan Doyle, grief-stricken at the death of his son in the First World War, attempted, in the latter part of his life, to establish contact with the boy.

The Bible describes life as a journey through a vale of tears. Early man sought to establish contact with his departed loved ones through a formidable continuation of this journey—into the dreaded realm of the shades. The first to search for his beloved in that awesome world was the Greek musician Orpheus.

From the story of Orpheus and his wife, William Congreve derived the expression, "Music hath charms to soothe a savage breast, to soften rocks, or bend a knotted oak." So beautiful was the playing of Orpheus on his lyre that ferocious beasts forgot their quarrels and lay down side by side. Even stones and trees were known to draw nearer, so powerful was the charm of his music.

For many years, Orpheus and Eurydice lived happily together in a beautiful vale in Thrace until the cold hand of Death intervened. Eurydice trod on a serpent and died of its venom. At first, Orpheus laid his lyre aside, too grief-stricken to do anything but mourn her loss. Then, in a desperate attempt to be reunited with his beloved Eurydice, he determined to venture into the Underworld and persuade its cold-hearted king, Hades, to permit Eurydice to return to the land of the living.

Taking his lyre, Orpheus wandered westward until he came to the gloomy cavern that leads tortuously in dark descent to the black waters of the River Styx, a name so dreaded that the gods use it only to bind a solemn and sacred oath.

Over the surface of the fathomless waters, a fog hung so thick that the ferry boat of the dread Charon, who transports the dead across Styx's icy waters, loomed suddenly before Orpheus. The eyes of Charon glared balefully at him. "Go back to the land of the living; this is the realm of Hades", his old voice quavered. Orpheus, however, by the magic of his lyre, persuaded Charon to take him to the other side.

Here he beheld a dismal place of waste and wild. So it must have been in the beginning when only Night and Erebus had emerged from Chaos. As Orpheus advanced cautiously, huge chasms gaped suddenly before him. Screams of souls in torment filled the void around him and chilled him to his very soul. Still he continued onward, singing of his past happiness and his hope of reunion with Eurydice.

Such was the power of his music that the thin shades, souls that had lost the power of memory when they drank of the waters of the River Lethe, now recalled the warmth of earth, the sunshine forever lost to them, and the happiness of love. As these thoughts flooded into their memories, the screams of those in torment ceased; Sisyphus no longer strained at his rock; and Ixion's wheel forgot to turn.[7] The marrow-chilling air of the Underworld seemed momentarily to warm, and the blackness to dispel, as Orpheus wandered farther and farther into the murky depths.

7. In punishment for betraying the secrets of the gods, Sisyphus had to strain perpetually against a huge rock; for a crime against Zeus, Ixion was bound to a fiery wheel which turned without ceasing. See Robert Graves, *The Greek Myths: I.*

Then he stood before the throne of Hades, grim and inhuman as the realm he ruled, with Persephone, his beautiful consort.

When the strains of the music reached Persephone, she bethought herself of the happy, carefree days in the sun-bathed fields of Enna in Sicily and of her mother for whom she longed. No sooner had Orpheus pleaded with Hades to spare Eurydice and allow her to return with him to the land of the living than Persephone turned to her husband and begged him to grant Orpheus his wish.

Moved by the power of Orpheus's music and the entreaties of Persephone, even the hard heart of Hades momentarily softened and he summoned Eurydice. Orpheus waited. His yearning of over twelve months was now to be answered.

When Eurydice appeared before them, even as a shade, she seemed to retain some of the radiance of her earthly form. Slowly and deliberately, Hades's voice enunciated the conditions under which he would allow Eurydice to accompany Orpheus to the fields of light: she was to follow Orpheus, who must show his trust in Hades by not looking back until he had reached the upper air.

With a light heart, Orpheus began the homeward journey, passing the pool of Lethe, crossing the River Styx, and ascending the winding path which led to the upper world. Just as he was nearing the end of his long, arduous journey and saw the gleam of the upper world ahead, doubt smote his buoyant spirit. What if Hades were deceiving him? What if Eurydice were still in the Underworld? For one frantic moment, he glanced over his shoulder. He had broken his bargain with Hades!

His horror-stricken eyes beheld the figure of Eurydice fading backward, farther and farther into the darkness. Her farewell murmur reached his ears. Then silence.

In vain, he plunged down the path in search of her, but this time Charon, acting on the orders of Hades, could not be prevailed upon to take him across the river.

The heartbroken Orpheus returned alone to the upper world. Soon, in death, he joined Eurydice in Hades's kingdom.

In memory of Orpheus, Apollo built a shrine on the island of Lesbos. There, it is said, the nightingales sing more beautifully than anywhere else in the world.

In Indian legend, too, friendship and love, temporarily cut off by death, are recorded. The main distinction between Indian stories concerning the afterlife and their Greek counterpart is that the Indian conception of the world beyond is not desolate and void of hope.

> Sunset and evening star.
> And one clear call for me!
> And may there be no moaning of the bar,
> When I put out to sea.
>
> But such a tide as moving seems asleep
> Too full for sound and foam,
> When that which drew from out the boundless deep
> Turns again home.
>
> Alfred, Lord Tennyson, "Crossing the Bar"

## The Boy in the Land of Shadows

Most accounts of the afterlife conceive of it as lying beyond a body of water: the River Styx, the River

Jordan, the river which Christian in *Pilgrim's Progress* had to cross before reaching the eternal city whence the trumpets sounded, or simply the ocean lying to the westward which we, like the dying sun, must cross at the end of our journey. Such is the Indian legend of the boy in the Land of Shadows.

So old is this legend[8] that the names of the boy and his sister have been forgotten. They were orphans, and dwelt alone in the mountains, remote from any tribe. In spite of this, they were happy; the boy provided food and raiment through his skill with the bow, the girl cooked and sewed. But, like Orpheus and Eurydice, their happiness together was short-lived. One cruel winter, so cold that the frost split the trees and the wilderness seemed a vast emptiness void of life, the boy, in spite of his tireless efforts, was unable to find game. The few roots that he succeeded in foraging were insufficient to keep the flame of life burning within his sister. One evening her soul slipped away on its westward journey.

Unable to endure living alone and amid scenes that constantly reminded him of his sister, the boy set out to find the happy land where dwell the spirits of the departed. His destination reached, he planned either to live there forever with his sister or to bring her back with him to their mountain home.

He carefully avoided an encounter with any of the strange tribes that he met on the way, and steadily

8. Norval Morriseau, in *Legends of My People, the Great Ojibway,* relates a similar story in which a boy searches for his younger brother who had died and gone to the Happy Hunting Grounds located here on earth, near Fort Frances.
There is also a Chipewyan legend concerning the "island of souls" in which a young man seeks for his betrothed in the land of the dead.

pursued his journey westward until he came to the Great Water.

There he met an old man on whose seamed and wrinkled face were recorded the many winters he had lived.

"What are you doing here?" the old man challenged.

The boy told of his sister's death and explained his quest.

The old man said, "You have undertaken a difficult and dangerous mission, but, provided you keep a stout heart, I will help you. Several moons ago, your sister came this way; now she has gone to the Land of Shadows in the Country of Silence, which lies out yonder in the Island of the Blest. There time, disease, sickness, and pain are unknown. In consequence, no one ever wearies or grows old. However, to get there, you must cross a turbulent sea."

Taking the boy by the hand, he led him to the shelter of a cove and pointed to a beautiful white canoe that had been hewn from one huge stone. Then he handed the youth a pouch of tobacco and a clay pipe, saying, "This you will have need of before you reach your journey's end."

Just as the evening star gleamed in the sky, the boy put out to sea. After he passed the headland, the waves rose higher and higher threatening to overwhelm his canoe, but it cleft through them unswervingly, as if guided to the lodestone of an unknown destination. In the sea around him the boy saw other canoes, white and shining like his own. All seemed to be set on the same course; but, to his amazement, none seemed to be occupied. The youth shouted across the tempest-tossed waters in the hope that a human voice would answer, but the only response was the roar of the waters and the howling of the wind. From time to time, a wave more mountainous than the others would seize a canoe and hurl it into the depths of the sea. Each time a craft disappeared into the angry waves, the boy thought he heard the cry of a soul in agony.

After several days, the sea grew calm and the air warm and sweet with the breath of blossoms. The boy looked around and realized that he was in the lee of an island. Grass, emerald-green, growing on gentle slopes, eventually merged into the crystal waters of the sea. Ahead, a beach, whiter than any he had ever seen, gleamed in the sun's warm rays. He had reached his destination—the Island of the Blest. After beaching his canoe, the youth strode along the sand. Suddenly he came upon a skeleton bleached white by long exposure to the sun.

As he looked down upon it, the skeleton sat up. "Why are you here?" it asked. "You should be in the land of the living."

After the boy told his story, the skeleton said, "I may be able to help you find your sister, but first let me smoke your pipe." As the skeleton puffed away, wisps of smoke drifting upward suddenly changed into white doves which flew before them. "Follow these," said the skeleton, "and you will find your sister."

The boy did as he was bid, and soon entered a glen fragrant with the aroma of pines. Thick beds of moss deadened his footfalls as he advanced through a forest which appeared to be deserted, although he heard the singing of birds. He was now in the Country of Silence.

Emerging from the forest, he heard voices. Yet he could not determine whence they came. Then he reached the entrance to a garden. Here the doves stopped, circled overhead and lighted on the branch of a tree—all except one, which perched on his shoulder. He had reached his destination, the Land of Shadows.

As he entered the garden, he heard once more the murmur of voices, but still he could see no human forms. Then on the grass he saw many shadows of people and realized with amazement that the shadows were speaking. Still he could see no one to give shape to these shadows. The sun itself seemed to be forming them.

As he listened more intently, the boy's heart leapt for joy. He heard a voice which he knew to be his sister's. Listening closely, he soon discerned the shadow from which the voice came.

He threw himself on the grass beside the shadow and joyfully spoke. "Long have I sought you, my beloved sister, that I may take you with me back to our home, which is sad and empty without you."

Sorrowfully, she replied, "I cannot go back with you now, for I have eaten the fruit of this land.[9] Had you come sooner, I could have returned; now it is impossible."

In vain, the youth tried to persuade her to come with him. In vain, he offered to stay there forever with her. She explained that he had his own life to lead; that he was destined to become a chief to his people; that he would be renowned, not for war, but for the pursuit of peace, for mercy shown to his enemies, and for sharing his goods with the less fortunate. He must fulfil his role in life before he could be permitted to

9. A tradition common to many myths; example, Demeter and
   Persephone

stay and share with her eternal youth and happiness amongst the blest.

The youth now knew where his duty lay. As he rose sorrowfully to depart, his sister said, "I shall give you this shadow. When it is with you, no evil can befall you, for it is present only in the light, and where there is light, evil cannot lurk. When the shadow has departed, darkness will surround you; then, Brother, be on your guard."

Bidding his sister farewell, the brother retraced his steps across the Country of Silence, embarking in his canoe and sailing this time across calm seas until he reached the cove whence he had begun his voyage.

The boy lived to an old man, and was loved and honoured by all. When he died, he vanished as the snow in spring, taking his shadow with him. His people knew that he was now with his sister in the Land of Shadows in the Island of the Blest.

There they live happily still. However, for a short time every year, they yearn to revisit the familiar scenes of their childhood. Then their spirits are allowed to come back to linger over the places they knew so well. At this time a hush descends on the land, now as still as the Country of Silence; and a silver haze, the smoke of their campfire, fills the air. We call this time Indian summer: it is a shadow of the golden summer that went before it. It is a reminder to the people that, when they die, they, too, will journey westward and enjoy a life of eternal youth in the Land of Shadows.

# 3
# A Sense
# of Wonder

Those who dwell, as scientists or laymen, among the beauties and mysteries of the earth are never alone or weary of life. Whatever the vexations or concerns of their personal lives, their thoughts can find paths that lead to inner contentment and to renewed excitement in living. Those who contemplate the beauty of the earth find reserves of strength that will endure as long as life lasts. There is symbolic as well as actual beauty in the migration of birds, the ebb and flow of the tides, the folded bud ready for spring. There is something infinitely healing in the repeated refrains of nature—the assurance that dawn comes after night, and spring after winter.

Rachel L. Carson, The Sense of Wonder

Laurens van der Post advanced the opinion that the savage, because he dwells among the beauties and the mysteries of the earth, has a deeper spiritual insight into the mystery of life surrounding him than the European, a product of a more advanced civilization:

One realises that it is not we who are filled with spirit or soul but rather the dark and despised people about us. They have so much of it that it overflows in trees, rocks, rivers, lakes, birds, snakes and animals that surround them. . . . But one and all they are humble parts of life and at one with it knowing that, in order to get through their tiny, trembling day, they are in constant need of support from a power greater than themselves.

Laurens van der Post, The Dark Eye in Africa

This overflow of spirit is evident in all primitive societies. The early Greeks, imbued with a sense of wonder on beholding the beauty and majesty of nature, endowed it with a host of supernatural creations: the oceans and streams were nymphs[1] and nereids; each tree had its own spirit, called a dryad; the hills and mountains were the abode of fauns.

The Indians had a similar concept of nature. When the first Indian, in what is now Yoho National Park, B.C., beheld the water plunging down the mountain, with such violence that its voice resembled a continuous roll of thunder, he cried, "Takakkaw", which means "O wonderful!". This word *wonderful* expressed the Indian's awe and submission before the Wonderful (and His name shall be called Wonderful), the Manitou, the Great Spirit who created the heavens and the earth, and who revealed himself through the majesty of his creations.

To the Indian, the mountains were not formed as a result of the enfolding of the earth's surface. The waterfalls were not products of the upheaval of nature. The rainbow was not made by the action of

---

1. Most famed of nymphs was Thetis, mother of Achilles. Thetis had the ability to transform herself into various creatures when the whim struck her.

light reflecting off water.[2] Rather, these were phenomena, the handiwork of the Creator. Many legends testify to the wonder of their creation.

Waterfalls, in particular, evoked the Indians' sense of the miraculous. Niagara Falls, with its mighty waters hurtling down the gigantic precipice; the Cave of the Winds, hidden behind a sheet of foaming water; the strange effects of the mist; the weird forms of the rocks sculpted through the centuries by the force of water—all these quickened the imagination of the Indians, particularly the Senecas and the Tuscaroras, who lived within range of these wonders.

Most of the Indian legends of Niagara Falls include a giant, the Cave of the Winds, and the "Maid of the Mist". In one story, narrated by Maxine in *L'Ogre de Niagara*, the giant created Niagara Falls. Under the spell of an evil medicine man, this giant and a beautiful Indian maiden had been imprisoned in a huge cavern—now the Cave of the Winds. After their rescue by a brave Indian youth, the giant diverted the flow of the Niagara River so that the torrent of water fell over the cliff, engulfed the wigwam of the medicine man, and destroyed him and all his tribe.

Here is another legend that speaks to us "with the odours of the forest, with the curling smoke of wigwams, with the rushing of great rivers and their wild reverberations."[3]


## Hinun, the Giant of Niagara Falls

There once lived a beautiful Seneca maid. She was

2. The rainbow was a wonderful bridge which first the deer and then the other animals climbed. They can now be seen as stars.
3. Henry Wadsworth Longfellow, *The Song of Hiawatha*

sought in marriage by many braves, any of whom would have made a good husband, since each was not only a skilful hunter but also noble and generous in spirit. For some reason unknown to the rest of the tribe, the maid's parents spurned these eligible suitors and gave their daughter to an old man whose purpose in life was the amassing of as much wealth as he could get his greedy hands on. Actually the old man was possessed of great power, but it was the power of evil, for wicked spirits had taken possession of his soul and it was they who had given him control over the girl's parents and induced them to part with their beloved daughter.

Forced to submit to the taunts and inhuman treatment of the old man, the luckless girl despaired of ever knowing a moment's happiness again. She was forced to toil from morn till night, day after day. On more than one occasion, she attempted to run away. Each time her husband, through some uncanny sense, seemed to have been forewarned of her plan and caught her. Each time, the punishment he imposed was harsher than before.

One evening, after the sun had departed on his journey to the west and the hunters had returned in their canoes, she momentarily evaded the watchful eye of the old man and slipped down to the shore of the river. Silent as a shadow, she slid the nearest canoe into the turgid waters. Once again, she was away.

At first she paddled frantically. Then her frail canoe touched the swift-moving current. Its bow swung downstream. Helpless in the clutch of the mighty river, it swept towards the waterfall, and, swift as an arrow in flight, shot over the precipice. In the split second the canoe plummeted down to the treacherous rocks below, the maiden anticipated the moment in which she would be dashed to her destruction.

Instead, to her amazement, she now felt herself lifted, as if by a giant hand that had caught her in flight. She found herself in a vast cavern, behind the torrent of water and reclining at the feet of a giant who towered high as the loftiest pine.

The giant looked down on her, his eyes filled with compassion.

"I am Hinun, the giant whose voice you have heard speaking from my home in the falls," he said. Long have I witnessed your suffering under the cruel hand of your husband, whose evil soul is possessed of the powers of greed and selfishness. Here you will find rest from your labour and peace from the torment that your spirit has undergone. Here you may remain until the old man dies."

For many seasons, the maid lived in the giant's cavern, where she enjoyed a contentment that she had not experienced since leaving the dwelling of her parents. The giant kept her advised of what was happening in the camp, and of how the old man had sought her far and wide before abandoning the search.

One day the giant came to her and said, "Each day the power of evil grows stronger within your husband. Now, in his craze for wealth, he has leagued himself with the white man. He bargains in the souls of his tribesmen, selling them the white man's whiskey for whatever price he can exact. The time has come for me to challenge this evil man, to destroy him utterly before his power spreads and completely chokes the life from your people."

So saying, the giant departed.

In the meantime, the old man was gloating over the furs which his evil trade had amassed him. Fondly he touched the glittering wampum he had exacted from his tribesmen. So intent was his preoccupation with his illgotten treasures, that he was unaware of the presence of Hinun until the giant's angry voice shattered the silence of the forest.

"Your hour of death has come, old man," he shouted. "No longer can the evil within you spread to infect others."

With a laugh, the old man replied, "I have no fear of you, for my power of evil is stronger than any puny power you may possess." Whereupon, he changed himself into a man of stone.

In vain, Hinun wrestled with him, endeavouring to hurl his powerful antagonist to the ground. Strive as he might, the giant was as a helpless child contending with an immovable object. Then Hinun leaped from the grasp of his adversary and sprang up on the huge rock above the waterfall. From this vantage point, he shot arrow after arrow, but without effect. Each was shattered as soon as it struck the invincible man of stone, who now advanced relentlessly until both assailants stood at the top of the precipice.

Then the old man seized Hinun and pushed him towards its edge. With a shout of triumph, he reached out his arms to hurl him down into the roaring waters. But Hinun slipped to one side. Unable to check his course, the old man plunged to his death. When he fell, his stone body was shattered into fragments of rocks.

Hinun restored the girl to her people and then entered the depths of the cave, never to be seen again. But the girl went to look on the scene of the contest between Hinun and her husband. Gazing downward at the rock fragments of her wicked husband, she noticed that they still bore a resemblance to the human form and said to those who were with her, "Let all who seek wealth and riches look down on these stones and take warning."

Whoever has visited Kakabeka Falls, north of Thunder Bay, has probably been told the story of Greenmantle, the lovely and courageous Ojibway maiden. Some people contend that this is not an Indian legend; however, it is in the *tradition*[4] of the legend in that it brings to life the ghosts of a past long faded: the embers of the campfire lighting the dusky figures gathered round it, the soft sound of moccasined feet gliding along forest trails, and the canoe slipping smoothly and silently through waters which mirror the dark forest.

## Greenmantle

It was near sundown. Lightly as a fawn, the Indian maiden moved beneath the giant spruces. Then, emerging from the woods, she darted up the hill that sheltered the forest. Now and then, she disappeared from view to become, like the woodland life around her, a part of nature.

At the summit of the hill, Greenmantle stood, slender as the aspen that graced the woodlands surrounding her father's encampment · near the thundering falls of the Kaministiquia. Today her steps had taken her far from the camp, far from her people, into the heart of the woodlands. But she sensed no danger. The forest through which she roamed at will was as much a part of her as the village in which she

4. A Cree legend concerning Iroquois Falls has many similarities to this legend.

had been born sixteen years ago. No danger lurked behind the massive spruce or the thick brush. Had not the last report to reach her people assured them that the Sioux[5] were many miles to the south? The birds, through whose medley of calls only the liquid notes of the white-throat could be distinguished, assured her that here she was welcome. Here she was among friends.

Suddenly, she leapt to one side, skirted a boulder that blocked her path, effortlessly descended the slope, and disappeared once more beneath the cover of the forest.

Without warning, a black cloud crossed the face of the slanting sun. As though an icy hand held the world in its grip, a cool breeze stirred through the forest. From a nearby pine, a bluejay screamed its warning. Then a pall of silence descended.

Greenmantle looked round her like a frightened doe scenting the wind; then she edged cautiously past the wraithlike trunks of the beeches that stood out palely against the forest darkness.

Ahead, the shadows opened. Three warriors, whose copper skins were covered with ochrous paint, advanced towards her. Transfixed with horror, she stood helpless for a moment, then ran into the depths of the forest. With a frenzied burst of speed, the Indian maiden almost succeeded in evading her pursuers. But sinewy arms reached out to seize her. Strong hands held her in their grasp.

---

5. Possibly the Cree; however, the Sioux were a nomadic people. Therefore they might well have been in this region. In David Thompson's *Narrative of His Explorations in Western America, 1784-1812* (Greenwood Reprint Corp.) an Ojibway chief speaks of the Sioux: "Until we have horses like them, we must keep to the woods, and leave the Plains to them."

In the semidarkness of the predawn, the indistinct form of a birchbark canoe moved out from the shadows on the edge of the Kaministiquia River. The rhythmic rise and fall of the paddles broke the calm of the mirror-like water. Between the silhouettes of two braves, was the shadowy form of Greenmantle, huddled in the centre of the boat. As the first canoe drifted towards the centre of the river, others slipped away from the shore until a small flotilla moved ghostlike through the water.

As the lead canoe moved into the looming darkness, the warriors trembled with the anticipation of surprising their quarry. Hadn't they forced a promise from the chief's daughter that she would guide them to the wigwams of her people? Greenmantle clenched her hands so tightly that the blood was drained from them. Sobs broke from her lips, as she offered up a prayer for the people whom she had betrayed.

The war party followed the serpentine form the Kaministiquia made between the hills. Darkness had partially lifted from the forest, and the shapes of individual trees could be distinguished. Greenmantle cast an anxious glance towards them; then, as if fearing detection, forced herself to look in the opposite direction. The lead canoe was rounding a wide bend in the river. Greenmantle stiffened. Her heart was pounding so loudly she feared that her captors would hear it. Surely they must see—their eyes, accustomed to following the faintest trail, could not fail to discern so obvious a sight—the wigwams of her people, huddled beneath the low brush which flanked the elbow of the river.

Rigid with fear, she scanned the opposite shore. The warriors' gaze followed hers, but their arms moved in regular rhythm as the paddles rose and fell.

Soon all the canoes had passed the village. Then a sound like the voice of thunder was carried to them by the light breeze that now stirred on the face of the water. Greenmantle's heart jumped. It was too late. Now the canoes were plunging forward. As though drawn by a giant hand, they were swept into the current. She had done it. She had kept her word. She had guided the enemy to the wigwams of her people, but, at the same time, she had become the saviour of her people. In a futile attempt to save themselves, the savages plunged their paddles into the swirling waters. Their frenzied screams drowned in the roar of the falls, as they were hurled into the depths below.

Today, where the Indian encampment used to be, a bridge spans the river. A park and tourist information bureau stand where virgin forest once witnessed the self-sacrifice of Greenmantle, the Indian heroine who saved her people but could not save herself.

It is said that the spirit of Greenmantle still roams the forest. And, if you look into the heart of the falls just as the sun's arrows are beginning to pierce the morning mist, you may see the outline of this beautiful and courageous maiden.

## Mountain and Rock Formation

The grand and the sublime in Nature are sources of wonder to man. The communities nestled at the foot of the Rocky Mountains or the Gaspésian elevations of eastern Canada appear as infinitesimal before the majesty and grandeur of God's creation.

To all people endowed with imagination, cloud formations are a source of wonder and speculation. Each of us has at some time gazed heavenward and seen—not clouds—but shapes: lions, lambs, ominous mushroom formations, flaming pillars, old men with flowing beards and windswept hair.

In the forests of Thessaly, Mount Olympus towers 9,000 feet above the neighbouring countryside, its peaks hidden by clouds. The ancient Greeks envisioned these lofty peaks as the homes of the gods.[6] Hidden from the view of man, Zeus, king of the gods, hurled his mighty thunderbolts earthward. Here the councils of the Olympian gods were held— councils that determined the fate of man. Mount Aetna in Sicily, with its turbulent and sulphurous volcanoes, was the home of the giant Cyclopes, the blacksmiths of the gods, who worked at their underground forges which belched forth flame and smoke.

For ancient peoples, stories might be read in rocks, too. The Atlas Mountains in North Africa came into being when the Greek hero Perseus, returning from his quest for the Gorgan's head, transformed the Titan Atlas, the sky bearer, into stone to relieve him of the dreadful pain caused by his heavy burden.[7] The two rocks on either side of the Strait of Gibraltar were the pillars of Hercules, placed there by that hero when he travelled to the kingdom of Geryon, to signify the end of the world.[8] A long black rock with the blue Mediterranean lapping at its base was not always a rock.

6. Nor were the Greeks unique in associating mountains with superhuman figures. Note the incredible snowman of the Himalayas.
7. For the story of Perseus and Atlas, consult Thomas Bulfinch, *The Age of Fable.*
8. Later, these two rocks were pictured as pillars, bound together by a scroll bearing the Latin words *ne plus ultra* which means *no more beyond.* This was a warning to sailors not to go into the Atlantic.

At one time, it was a huge and terrifying monster changed into stone by the Greek hero Perseus, just as it was about to devour a beautiful maiden named Andromeda.[9] Reefs in the Mediterranean near Sicily, often the destruction of unfortunate vessels, were once beautiful maidens called "Sirens",[10] who enticed passing sailors with their enchanting singing, only to devour them and leave their bones to bleach in the sun.

Corresponding to Hercules is Glooscap, the god of the Micmacs. Anyone travelling by automobile along the Nova Scotia coastline will see strange rock formations in the water. These were hurled into the ocean by Glooscap in a fit of anger. One circular rock is Glooscap's tea-kettle. A cleft rock was formed when Glooscap hurled his thunderbolt at the dam erected by Beaver who, in league with Malsumsis,[11] the evil brother of Glooscap, had made this huge dam in order to dry up the streams and destroy Glooscap's people. A similar explanation is given to account for the islands along the British Columbia coast. These were formed when a mighty eagle, possibly a thunderbird, flung the bodies of all the males of a tribe into the ocean in punishment for their shooting arrows at him.

9. See R.S. Lambert, "Perseus and Andromeda", and "The Labours of Hercules", *Myths, Legends and Fables.*

10. The Sirens appear in R.S. Lambert, "Jason and the Argonauts" and "The Home-Coming of Odysseus", *Myths, Legends and Fables.*

11. In much the same manner as told in the Nordic cycle, Malsumsis tried to find out what weapon or growing thing would kill Glooscap.

*The Legend of Siwash Rock*[12]

In Burrard Inlet, off Vancouver's Stanley Park, a column of rock towers, a fringe of brush at its crest and a long pine pointing from its summit into the sky. Barren and rough-hewn, it stands amidst the changing pattern of modern ocean traffic, a silent testimony to the permanence of nature's creations. Appropriately, it is called Stanley Park's "Sentinel".

This rock is a monument, built, not by man but by God, in tribute to what the Indians regarded as the spirit of unselfishness dwelling within the heart of man.

Its origin is shrouded in the mists of Time; hence, accounts of its creation vary. One of the most beautiful legends surrounding it is the following:

Thousands of years ago, there dwelt amongst the Squamish tribe of the coastal region a chieftain, T'elch, famed throughout the region for his good deeds. Blest by the creator with strength and wisdom, with a beautiful and gentle wife, strong sons, and skill in hunting and fishing, he wanted nothing for himself and bestowed the bounty which heaven had given him upon those less fortunate than he was.

One day, the village was astir with anticipation which spread from lodge to lodge like the fresh breath of returning spring. The Squamish people were going to be visited by the Changer. Now when the Changer honours a tribe with his presence, he grants to each person whatever he may request. Hence the excitement was understandable. Each member of the tribe was ready with his request—good fortune in the hunt,

---

12. A different account is given in E. Pauline Johnson, *Legends of Vancouver*.

strong sons to succeed him, long days on earth void of the crippling onset of old age. Each member except T'elch. Since he had already been blest with so much, T'elch did not intend to ask for anything.

Early in the morning of the long-awaited day, T'elch plunged into the cool waters of what is now called Burrard Inlet. With strong strokes, he swam vigorously out to sea. If the Changer were going to honour his tribe with his presence, he, T'elch, must be prepared—he must be pure, and water was the great purifier, both of body and the soul.

T'elch had been swimming for several minutes when he saw, in the distance, what appeared to be a canoe. As it neared him, it loomed larger and larger, almost blocking the rays of the slanting sun, which rested on the surface of the deep. Four paddles dipped in unison, four figures of gigantic stature leaned forward. So great was its speed that it seemed to part the surface of the water. Then the tallest and stateliest of the four men, he who steered the canoe, rose to his full height and addressed T'elch in a mighty voice.

"I am the Changer. What is your wish? Speak. For whatever it may be, it shall be granted."

T'elch ceased swimming. Although awed by the mighty presence before him, he did not hesitate to reply, "I do not wish to ask anything for myself, for I have already been blest far beyond what I deserve."

A smile like the rays of the morning sun illuminated the countenance of the Changer and he spoke in a gentler tone.

"In our journey around the world, we have met no one but you who has been free from selfishness. We want you to stand for all time as a monument so that those who look on you will realize that they too should be unselfish."

T'elch grew in stature, and was transformed into the gigantic stone pillar that stands, tall and erect, in Burrard Inlet, a perpetual reminder of an unselfish chieftain.

Pauline Johnson was so impressed by the beauty of this legend that she asked that when she died her body be cremated and the ashes scattered on the water in front of Siwash Rock. A headstone has been placed in her memory at English Bay, overlooked by Prospect Point where a large totem pole has been erected.

## The Sleeping Giant

Whoever has visited the twin cities of the Lakehead, Fort William and Port Arthur, has seen the "Sleeping Giant". This unique formation, which seems at once so near the busy life of the urban community of Thunder Bay, and yet so remote, is cut off from the mainland by the waters of Lake Superior. Silhouetted against the skyline in dramatic contrast to the sky-reflecting blue of Thunder Bay, it has the shape of a giant lying prone on the rock surface, the arms folded across the chest. The facial features and the headdress identify the figure as an Indian chief at rest.

To appreciate fully the story of the Sleeping Giant, Nanna Bijou, one must disregard the discordant sounds of commercial, twentieth-century life and return, in spirit, to the era before the coming of the white man, when the Indian roamed, unmolested, the forests of this big country.

The story begins, not in the Lake Superior region, but near Niagara Falls where Nanna Bijou lived with his grandmother, Nokomis.[13] Nanna Bijou did not

13. Nokomis is the Ojibway word meaning *grandmother*.

know who his parents were. Nokomis said that he had been sent by the sky-people to be the saviour of his people. However, as his people dwelt in peace and happiness, young Nanna Bijou had no idea what he was to save them from.

At an early age, it was apparent that the boy was not the same as other boys. He asked questions of his elders which indicated that he far excelled the other youths of the tribe in wisdom. As he grew older, his stature, strength and skill at games surpassed the strongest of the braves. He was at one with the creatures of the forest; even the most timorous, the rabbits and the fawns, drew near at his approach. The corn he planted waved in the breeze over the heads of the highest planted by others. With this evidence that the sky-people looked favourably upon Nanna Bijou, his tribesmen naturally looked up to him as their leader.

One summer a change took place in the boy. Hitherto, Nanna Bijou had been of a happy, carefree nature, cheerful as the sun which shone down on him and seemed to bless his every action. Now, he no longer sought the company of others, but sat apart and brooded in the wilderness and solitary places.

This change alarmed Nokomis. Then, in response to her entreaties, Nanna Bijou said: "A message has been sent to me in a dream warning me of the doom of my people.[14] A giant canoe, ten times bigger than any war canoe that I have ever seen came from the direction of the rising sun. Even stranger than its

14. Glooscap of the Micmacs also had a vision of the coming of the white man. This vision signified not only the decline of the red man but also the waning of Glooscap's powers. Sadly, Glooscap bade farewell to his people, embarked in his canoe, and paddled towards the departing sun.

immense size was its movement. Not a paddle broke the surface of the water, yet it moved silently and steadily westward, as though guided by some gigantic, invisible hand. Above the canoe, were spread huge white wings, ready for flight. The men in the canoe were not brown like us, but white as the snows of winter. Hair grew on their faces. Their speech was strange. I could not understand what they were saying.

"Then the dream changed. I saw these same men spreading terror and destruction in our villages. Soon our people were driven from their lands. I have seen a vision warning me that the days of the red man in this land are numbered, but there is nothing I can do about it. I seek the solitary places in the hope that Gitche Manitou will tell me how to save my people."

Shortly after revealing his dream to Nokomis, Nanna Bijou left the village. He journeyed far into the forest to pray and fast. This time he was gone much longer than he had ever been before. Then, just when Nokomis despaired of seeing him again, Nanna Bijou returned to the lodges of his people. He was gaunt and worn from his long sojourn, but, even before he uttered a word, the radiant light in his eyes proclaimed to his tribesmen that Gitche Manitou had revealed to him his course of action.

Eager and curious, Nanna Bijou's people gathered round him. Then, in a voice strong and resounding so that even those in the outer fringes of the awaiting multitude could hear, he spoke these words:

"For days I wandered in the forest ere I emerged onto the high place that overlooks the restless waters rushing towards the precipice. Here, on the second night, a voice spoke unto me, addressing me as the saviour of my people. Soon the white men will be in our villages, destroying and plundering, driving our people into the forest. To save you from this fate, I am to lead you to a new land, far to the north, and beyond the reach of the greedy white man. There we are to build new lodges and dwell in peace and harmony."

Some of the tribesmen assembled there derided Nanna Bijou. Slothful and set in their ways, fearful of venturing into regions remote from the land that had been theirs for generations, they scoffed, "Who is Nanna Bijou to proclaim himself the saviour of his people? Surely he is a false prophet leading us to our destruction to feed his own pride. Heed him not. Here we were born; here we will remain."

Nanna Bijou and Nokomis gathered the few possessions they could carry and set out on the long journey through the wilderness that they must endure before reaching the land Gitche Manitou had promised them. Most of the tribe showed faith in their leader by taking up their possessions and following him. Those who did not, true to Nanna Bijou's prediction, were soon driven from the land they had so stubbornly clung to; most of them perished in the wilderness.

Guided by Nanna Bijou, the faithful followers were miraculously spared, from the dangers that surrounded them by day and the unknown terrors that threatened by night, as they made their way along the shore of the huge inland lake past lands of hostile tribes. Fish, berries, and nuts in abundance, the gifts of the wilderness, saved them from starvation.

At last, they came to the region of the north where lay the home that Gitche Manitou had promised them. Here mountains, so high that their shoulders thrust into the cover of clouds, rose above turbulent rivers. From the mountain peaks, thunder rumbled, continuous as the mighty roar of Niagara's cataract. Lightning flashed earthward splitting huge balsams and pines.

Before their terrified eyes, a gigantic, screaming thunderbird[15] swooped down. They huddled together, looking to Nanna Bijou for deliverance.

Nanna Bijou stepped forward. "Be not afraid," he said to his tribesmen. "This is Thunderbird, sent by Gitche Manitou to lead us to our new home." He stretched forth his arm. Lo! the thunder and lightning ceased; the bird flew to his shoulder and perched there.

Thunderbird guided them to an island set in a bay which they appropriately called Thunder Bay, part of the great inland water the Indians named Gitche Gumee, the Big Sea Water, but which the white man has called Lake Superior.

For several years after they had reached this promised land, Nanna Bijou led his people in the ways of peace. Thunderbird had told him of a rich deposit of silver that underlay the coating of rock and earth placed there to conceal it from other wandering tribes. Nanna Bijou revealed this knowledge only to his closest friends. Together they mined the silver and hid it in a huge underground cave.

However the period of tranquillity enjoyed by Nanna Bijou's people was brief as Indian summer. A wandering Sioux who had been given shelter and food by the Ojibways overheard two of Nanna Bijou's friends talking about the silver. Possessed by greed and unmindful of the hospitality he had enjoyed, his

15. The thunderbirds were demigods in the Ojibway mythology. The Ojibway believed in two kinds of thunderbirds: one had an ordinary bill or beak, the other had a long, crooked beak. The latter, which the Ojibway believed had a very bad temper, made the louder noise and destroyed Indians by lightning; the former was of mild temper and did not make very much noise. See Norval Morriseau, *Legends of My People, the Great Ojibway.*

only thought was to obtain the wealth that lay stored beneath the rocks. Then he heard the word "shuniah"[16] (silver) spoken again, together with the revelation that, should the white man learn the secret of the silver, it would mean the end of the Ojibways' peaceful sojourn in the land of Gitche Manitou and the death of their tribe. In the greed-crazed mind of the Sioux, the course was clear. He would betray this knowledge to the white men in the south, and lead them to the hidden wealth. In turn, they would reward him with silver enough to make him rich and powerful.

Meanwhile, in a dream, Nanna Bijou had been warned of what was about to happen. Calling his people around him, he proclaimed in a sad voice:

"I have dreamed a dream in which I saw a canoe skimming over the water towards us like a gigantic sea bird. In it were the strange white men of whom I told you before. In this dream, Thunderbird spoke, commanding that you take all your possessions down into the caves below the mountains on the mainland, for Gitche Manitou will cause a mighty storm to move upon the surface of the waters. You are to remain in the caves until the waters cease their roar and the sun touches them once again. Then you are to gather your possessions and go to the rivers and lakes farther north, since this land will be yours no longer."

With eyes filled with love and compassion for the people he had led for so many years, Nanna Bijou continued, "This time I will not lead you on your journey. The time has come when I must leave you. Do as you have been taught, and Gitche Manitou will always be with you."

The great storm came. Gitche Manitou breathed on the surface of the waters, creating waves that rose

16. "Shuniah" is also money; in Cree, "soonias".

higher and higher until their foaming crests almost reached the sky. With his mighty hand, he bent the mountains until they bowed before the fury of the waters that lashed their base. The roar of the wind, the tumult of the Big Sea Water and the crashing of giant trees split by mighty thunderbolts rent the air. Amidst the seething waters, the boat of the greedy white men was but a toy. All the white men perished. Then, having accomplished their purpose, the waters grew calm, the clouds dispersed, and the gleaming surface of the bay blinked in the warm rays of the gentle sun.

The Indians emerged from their shelters and looked around them. Over the island which had been their home lay the gigantic form of Nanna Bijou, now at peace, looking upward towards the sky whence he had come.

With the death of the invading white men, perished the knowledge of the store of silver that lies beneath the surface of the rock. Still guarding that secret, lies the body of Nanna Bijou. There, the Indians say, he will remain until Gitche Manitou wakens him, when he will cross the broad river to the Great Beyond, or Place of the Dead.

The legend of the twin sisters depicts three aspects of the Indian character that the historian tends to overlook. The first is the Indians' respect for the peace-maker.[17] Though fierce and valorous in war, the

17. Not only legend, but history bears this out. The Five Nations (federation), conceived by the prophet, Deganoweda, and made a reality by Hiawatha, was called "The Great Peace". Its main principles were peace between individuals and tribes, right conduct and thought and justice and respect for human rights. Though the federation involved only five nations (later six), its founders hoped to extend it until all tribes were included. Oliver La Farge, *A Pictoral History of the American Indian*

Jackson Beardy '73

Indian, like Cincinnatus, famed in Roman story, was ever ready to lay down his weapons and take up the instruments of peace. The second is respect for women. The white man's conception of the Indian woman as being merely the chattel of the husband is all too prevalent. Amongst some tribes, the life of the woman was one of unbearable drudgery, but this was not true of every tribe. Usually a close bond existed between husband and wife. Until contemporary times, women of the tribes comprising the Five Nations of the Iroquois had more voice in administering the affairs of the nation than did white women of any country; for, though the women did not rule, the matrons chose the sachems, or chiefs, who represented the tribes at the council. They also had the power to recall or dismiss chiefs who had proved unsatisfactory. A third aspect of Indian life portrayed in this legend is participation, or involvement, as exhibited in the potlatch. Everyone in the tribe took part in this festival. All the guests had to be housed and fed for the fourteen to twenty-eight days' duration of the festivities. In addition, the entire host-tribe, even the children, had a role to play—hunting for the game, preparing the food for the feasts, gathering and piling the firewood, or participating in the plays, songs, and other entertainment. Even though the guest-tribe would have to hold the potlatch at a later date, the event typified the joy the Indians took in sharing their possessions.[18]

## The Legend of the Twin Sisters

This legend is told by the Indians of the British Columbia coast. Long ago, some say thousands of

18. See George Clutesi, *Potlatch*.

years ago, war's cruel hand laid hold of the tribes inhabiting the west coast of what is now British Columbia, and caused them to engage in fierce and bloody battles. The main opponents in these wars were the tribe dwelling in the region of the Capilano Canyon and the tribe living amongst the fjords and islands of the northern coast where the city of Prince Rupert now stands. Like all wars, this was a foolish war, for both tribes worshipped the same Great Spirit, the Sagalie Tyee, who had blessed them both by providing them with ample means to obtain a livelihood: from the salmon,[19] a never-ending source of food that each spring braved rapids and even leapt falls in their journey upstream; from the fruits that grew in the fertile valleys; and from the animals that abounded in the forests. Yes, the Sagalie Tyee had been good to them; but both tribes, like selfish children, instead of living in brotherhood and harmony, sought to keep the other from hunting and fishing in the coastal region.

The time came when the twin daughters of the chief of the southern tribe reached womanhood. This was an occasion that called for much rejoicing, for the Indians regarded the miracle of birth as the supreme gift of the Great Spirit, and gave honour to the mother, the fount of life.[20] It was through her that the tribe

19. The Indians held the salmon in special honour. It was not only a reliable source of food, but also had the ability to live an infinite number of lives. Every spring, the salmon swam up the rivers to breed (and then to die). The Indians did not realize that the young parr which later swam down to the ocean were salmon.

20. Amongst the early Greeks, woman's role in creation was held in such esteem that matriarchies prevailed. The early kings, having performed their function in procreation, were sacrificed to the gods. Evidences of such practices can be seen in stories describing the deaths of young males such as

survived: valiant sons were born to defend the tribe, gentle daughters to give it life.

The southern chief was determined to make this occasion a great celebration, for he loved and cherished his daughters as a special gift from the Sagalie Tyee, which indeed they were. Endowed by him with unequalled grace and beauty and having been nurtured in the Capilano Canyon remote from war's cruel slaughter, they grew up not only beautiful and radiant as the sunrise but also meek and pure in heart.

Summoning all the elders and chief warriors of his tribe, the southern chief announced that he was going to hold a big potlatch. He bade his people prepare food and special costumes for this event.

Weary of war, which had long darkened the land like a heavy cloud, the people responded joyfully to the chief's wishes. They busied themselves in making masks for the ritual dances; preparing food; and fashioning beads and ornate carvings, gifts for the maidens to be honoured.

Meanwhile the daughters witnessed the preparations made in their honour, not with gladness but with sorrow. As was their custom, they first took their problems to the Great Spirit, the Sagalie Tyee, praying to him at the foot of the mountains which rose from the forests bordering their home.

They then went to their father with a request that they scarcely dared hope he would grant. The taller of the two girls spoke:

"Father, we appreciate all that you have done for us

Hyacinthus, Orpheus, Dionysus, and Actaeon; and the prominence given to the worship of the moon-goddess, Artemis, before she was supplanted by Apollo. (See Robert Graves, *The Greek Myths: I*, pages 13-24, and Mary Renault's interesting novel *The King Must Die*, Pocket Books.)

in the past, and are doing to honour us now. Nevertheless our hearts can never be made glad unless you grant to us this, our request."

"O daughters, graceful as the aspen, beautiful with the beauty of sunrise, and gentle as the fawn, speak. What is your wish, that I may grant it?"

Again, the taller sister spoke, this time with greater assurance. "Father, we have now reached womanhood. Soon we shall be married and shall bear sons worthy to be called your grandchildren. But of what use is this if they are merely to be sacrificed to the cruel war that is casting its shadow over our land? We pray you, invite our brothers of the north to this, our festival, that they, too, may share our joy."

Amazed that they should even suggest bringing their enemies into the camp, the chief at first refused. But, when he realized that he could not bring them to his point of view, he granted them their wish.

Canoes were despatched into the regions held by the northern tribe. This time the young braves of the south bore, not weapons of destruction, but the invitation to attend the feast of the chief's daughters.

The warriors of the north responded in good faith. They cast aside their bows and arrows and war paint. Accompanied by their wives and children, and provided with stores of food and appropriate gifts, they set out on the southward journey.

The next few weeks witnessed the intermingling of the two tribes. Children of the north frolicked with their southern playmates on the beaches; as they prepared food for the festivities, the women of both tribes talked freely, as women do when they get together. The only rivalry exhibited among the men was in the stories they exchanged as they sat before the campfires.

Such festivities took place as had never been seen before. The tribes vied with each other in seeing who could offer the most food; games and contests were engaged in from dawn to sunset; singing and dancing continued until the pale finger of dawn touched the eastern rim of the sky.

But, just as day must yield to night and spring to summer, all things, even occasions as joyful as this, must have an end. The time came when the people of the south lined the shore to bid farewell to their northern comrades. As the canoes slipped away, the cries of "Farewell Brother" and "Good-bye, Hunter of the North" echoed across the still surface of the water in the early dawn.

From that day forth, the tribes of our western coast have lived in peace and harmony, for what man can wage war with his brother? Who can quarrel with his friend?

And the Sagalie Tyee, having seen all that had happened, was content. How best could he reward the twin sisters who had been responsible for bringing peace to a land so long torn by war? He wished to build a memorial to them that would stand forever as a testimony to their gentle and selfless spirits.

The Sagalie Tyee took them in his hands and set them high on the crest of the mountains overlooking Capilano Canyon. There they stand to this day, in the full glory of their youth, unwearied by age, unwrinkled with years. Just as the Sagalie Tyee had given them beauty and grace in their human form, so he now placed on their peaks a wreath of snow. Each day the sun changes at random the pattern of colours and tones—now vivid under his direct rays, now subdued by a soft cover of cloud, now veiled by pearly mists. Evening clothes them in rosy hues and night lends them her blanket of silver moonlight.

## Flowers and Plants

> I sometimes think that never blows so red
> The Rose as where some buried Caesar bled;
> That every Hyacinth the Garden wears
> Dropt in her Lap from some once lovely Head.
>
> Edward FitzGerald, *The Rubaiyat of Omar Khayyam*

In legend, fountains and waterfalls, because of their beauty and purity, are associated with lovely maidens. In both legend and song, flowers are thought of as springing from the blood of a young man or maiden. We use the metaphor even today when we speak of some one as having been "cut off in the flower of his youth".

Early legends conceive of plants having human attributes. In European myths, the mandrake, often associated with magic and sorcery, was believed to scream in pain when pulled from the earth. According to J.G. Frazer, the Indians, too, believed that plants and trees had souls. They believed, for example, that when the Missouri was swollen by a spring freshet which eroded its banks and uprooted tall trees, the spirits of these trees cried and their roots clung to the land until the trunks crashed into the stream and were swept away.[21]

The attributing of human characteristics to objects such as plants and trees is not confined to early or primitive societies. In *The Unexplained* Allen Spraggett affirms that tests have been made which prove that prayer has a positive effect on the growth of wheat. Such a theory implies that there is a force within the grain receptive to the human mind.

21. J.G. Frazer, *The Golden Bough*

The idea of the metamorphosis of a human being into a plant has a universal appeal, and stories narrating the transformation of a beautiful youth into a flower have become a part of the mythology of every race. From a host of such stories in Greek and Indian mythology, the following have been chosen.

## Hyacinthus

Since the sun is the source of all life on this planet, its warm rays unfolding the buds; awakening the seeds that lie dormant in winter's cold earth; and filling with teeming life, the land, sea, and air, the god of the sun played a dominant role in early religions.[22] In Greek mythology, Apollo, resplendently clothed in light, as befits the sun, was the god of medicine, and the divine inspiration for all the creative arts. Endowed with physical and spiritual beauty, he was foremost in the hierarchy of the gods.

At one time, there lived in Sparta a handsome prince named Hyacinthus, who, having found favour with Apollo, was blest with exceptional skill in performing athletic feats. On many occasions, Apollo descended to the earth to participate with him in sports.

This happy life shared by god and mortal came to an abrupt end. One day Apollo was teaching Hyacinthus to throw the discus. The west wind, resentful of Apollo's preoccupation with a mortal, caught the discus in flight and dashed it against

22. Foremost of the sun-worshippers were the Egyptians, whose hymn to Aten, or Re, the Sun-God, best expresses this veneration. Some scholars think that their beliefs were carried across the ocean to the Aztecs, whose religion, with its pyramids and its emphasis on sun-worship, is similar to that of the Egyptians.

Hyacinthus's skull. All of Apollo's skill in medicine was of no avail; helplessly, with tears in his eyes, the god bade farewell to his friend, who died in his arms.

Where the soil soaked up the blood of his friend, Apollo caused a hyacinth to spring forth as a lasting memorial. On its petals can be traced the initial letter of his name, Hyacinthus.

## Adonis

Another young man who died before the years had robbed him of his beauty was Adonis, so handsome that Aphrodite, goddess of love and beauty, was irresistibly attracted to him. Knowing his delight in hunting, she often invited him to join her in the chase. One day, while they were hunting wild boar on Mount Lebanon, the war god Ares, jealous of Aphrodite's love for Adonis, disguised himself as a wild boar. Charging out of a thicket, he ripped a savage gash in Adonis's thigh.

With blood spurting from his wound, Adonis sank to the ground. Before the horrified eyes of his beloved Aphrodite, he died, his spirit descending to the dark realm of Pluto and Persephone.

Aphrodite held Adonis in her arms, but his blood continued to flow, darkening the ground where it fell. From the drops of blood, beautiful red flowers began to grow. Delicate and fragile, their petals are scattered by the wind, hence their name—the anemone, or windflower.

Tearfully, Aphrodite begged Zeus to allow Adonis to return from the lonely land of the shades for half the year so that he might be her companion during the spring and summer.

This request Zeus granted. Every year, just as the

days are beginning to lengthen and the plants to put forth their shoots, Adonis returns to the world of light. Festivals are held to honour his return, and baskets of flowers flung into the river Adonis. Every year, so it is said, Adonis is slain by the boar. At this time, the river runs red with his blood. Then the people shout, "Farewell, Adonis, and may your return next year bring us as bountiful a harvest as this year's."[23]

Many other classical myths associate blood or death with plant or flower life. Narcissus, a youth who fell in love with his own face reflected in a pool, wasted away, and was transformed into a flower which we call the narcissus. According to the Roman poet Ovid, the berries of the mulberry changed from white to red after the blood of two young lovers, Pyramus and Thisbe, had soaked through the soil into the roots.[24]

## The First Fire-Flowers

In Indian legend, fire-flowers, which grow in such abundance that they sometimes blanket entire hillsides with their red blossoms, sprang from the blood of courageous young warriors. This is the story.

Thousands of years ago, fierce conflicts between the

23. Some version of the Adonis story, symbolic of the death and rebirth of vegetation, is represented in most cultures. Osiris and Tammuz are the Egyptian and Mesopotamian counterparts of Adonis. An Indian myth called "A Boy's Vision and the First Corn" is of similar nature, involving the death of the spirit of corn, Mondawmin, and his resurrection the following spring. This story is narrated in Ella Elizabeth Clark, *Indian Legends of Canada*.
24. "Echo and Narcissus" and "Pyramus and Thisbe" are narrated in Thomas Bulfinch, *The Age of Fable*.

southern tribes and those of the north raged up and down the coastal regions of British Columbia, their dispute centring over the possession of an island, now called the Island of Dead Men. Its name is appropriate, for, at one time, the waters encircling it ran red with the blood of the slain.

At last, the southern tribes lured the northern warriors far out to sea. Then, in their absence, a war party of the south returned under cover of night; raided the enemy camps; seized the women, the children and the old men too feeble for battle; and carried them to the Island of Dead Men.

When they realized that they had been duped by their enemy, the warriors of the north, in rage and frustration, launched wave after wave of war canoes upon the island in a valiant attempt to rescue their loved ones. The air was filled with arrows, the shrieks and lamentations of the imprisoned, and the groans of the dying. At first, the waves of northern warriors seemed to strike in vain; again and again, they were repulsed, only to gather force once more in a desperate onslaught on the foe. But after persistent attacks, one of the bravest and most respected of the southern warriors lifted up his hand and shouted across the waters:

"O men of the north, long have we stood up against you, but your numbers are greater than ours. Each day, there are fewer of us. Each day, our food supplies grow less, for in addition to ourselves, we are feeding our prisoners—your fathers and mothers, wives, and children. Hear, then, the terms which we, though weakened by battle, are still able to enforce. We will fight on, whatever your decision. Tomorrow we will kill all our prisoners. The only way that you can save them is by giving for each prisoner one of your bravest, strongest warriors. These will be put to death in their stead. Are you willing to accept these terms in order to save those you love?"

From the ring of northern canoes encircling the embattled warriors of the south arose a confusion of voices.

"I do not care what happens to me, but spare my young son."

"Let my daughter go free. I will willingly die in her place."

"Take me, but spare my father."

From the many who offered themselves, 200, the bravest and the best, were chosen.

In deference to the courage displayed by these valiant warriors, the circle of canoes fortifying the island gave way to allow them passageway to the shore. Here they stepped forth, shoulders erect, heads high, eyes flashing defiance at the enemy.

Honouring their part of the compact, the southern warriors quickly herded the old men, women, and children into the canoes. Some tried in vain to break from the strong arms of their captors, preferring to

join their husbands or sons in death rather than live without them.

Forming a long line before the southern warriors, these valiant young men bent down, only for a moment, to lay their bows and arrows at their feet. Then they stood, erect and unflinching, to await death.

The next morning, when the people of the south returned to the scene of havoc which they had wrought, they found that hundreds of brilliant flowers the colour of blood has sprung up overnight. The Sagalie Tyee had placed them there in honour of the fallen warriors.

This is the origin of the fire-flower, an everlasting remembrance of these valiant northern warriors, which now adorns the hills and wooded areas of our land.


## *The Lily*

The lily, like the anemone, hyacinth, and narcissus, has inspired many stories. One Indian myth tells how a star fell in love with the people of the earth.[25] She longed to dwell where she could see the children at play and look at the happy faces of the earth's early inhabitants. One spring morning, she slipped away from her accustomed position in the heavens. Drifting quietly downward, she hovered over the water, and then settled on its still, polished surface. Here, as a delicate white, star-shaped flower, she gained her wish. She could see the Indians as they drifted by in their canoes and hear the children playing on the shore.

25. This is told in an Ojibway legend. See Ella Elizabeth Clark, "The first white water lily", *Indian Legends of Canada*.

## The Spirit Sacrifice

Another Ojibway legend originated in the region of St. Mary's Falls, near Lake Superior. A plague which had swept over that part of the country had taken the lives of thousands of people. In order to appease the angry spirits responsible for the dread disease, a fitting sacrifice had to be offered—the life of the most beautiful girl in the tribe.

Sorrowfully, the women of the tribe prepared the maiden for sacrifice, dressing her in white robes, adorning her hair with flowers, and placing about her neck a string of rainbow-hued wampum beads. The canoe was made ready and, just as the rays of the sun slanted across the river, she was about to embark on her final journey over the falls, whose mighty voice shattered the evening stillness.

At that moment, above the roar of the water and the laments of her friends, a thin, clear, phantom voice was heard. Even the warriors were frightened. They stared about them, trying to find the source of the sound. Then, between them and the blood-red sun, a shadow floated. As it moved closer and closer, the form of a canoe took shape. This canoe moved without paddles, drawn towards them as by magic. In it sat a beautiful maiden clad in a robe of purest white. The sweet, clear tones of her song echoed across the river:

> I am come from the Spirit-Land
> To soften the wrath of the spirits.
> I come to stop the plague
> And save the life of the beautiful girl.[26]

The canoe drifted into the swift current, and was speedily carried to the brink of the precipice where it hovered momentarily before plunging downward. Engulfed in the foaming waters, it was seen no more.

The Ojibway Indians say the water lilies, white as snow, that fringe the St. Mary's River, are reminders of the beautiful maiden, the spirit-sacrifice, who took the place of the Ojibway maiden and saved the village from the dreaded plague.

26. The idea of a substitute for human sacrifice, common to most religions, shows the development of a reluctance to offer human sacrifice: cf. the golden ram substituted for Helle and Phrixus in Greek mythology. The story of Helle and Phrixus is told at the beginning of Edith Hamilton, "The Quest for the Golden Fleece", *Mythology*.

*Trees*

The day's long troubles lose their sting and pass.
Peaceful the world and peaceful grows my heart.
> Archibald Lampman, "A Summer Evening"

In the hush of the forest, a sense of harmony pervades the solitary walker. As he ventures into the vastness, a carpet of pine-needles deadens his footfalls. The pungent incense of cedar fills his nostrils; the trees stretching heavenward seem as giant pillars supporting the sky. At such moments, he senses the presence of the Creator of all things.

Pines shall Thy pillars be,
Fairer than those Sidonian cedars brought
By Hiram out of Tyre, and each birch-tree
Shines like a holy thought.
> Marjorie Pickthall, "Père Lalemant"

To primitive man, the forest was a mysterious and supernatural force. At the sacred grove in Upsala, the old religious capital of Sweden, every tree was regarded as divine. The Druids of early Britain performed their occult rites in the oak forest because they associated the oak with magic. In Greek mythology, the oak-grove at Dodona was sacred to Zeus. Here Athena obtained the speaking timber which she fitted into the prow of the *Argo* before Jason and his crew set forth in search of the Golden Fleece.[27] The Indians, too, associated trees with supernatural forces.

Having endowed trees with divine powers, primitive man required little imagination to give them human traits. Homer depicted the similarity between

27. Apollodorus, *The Library*, p. 97, translated by J.G. Frazer, The Loeb Classical Library

trees and men:

> As is the life of the leaves, so is that of man. The wind
> scatters the leaves to the ground; the vigorous forest
> puts forth others, and they grow in the spring season.
> Soon one generation of men comes and another
> ceases.
>
> *The Iliad*, Book VI

In most mythologies, trees were readily identified as people; in fact, they were people who had been changed by the gods into their present form.

Since trees provide man with many benefits— shelter from the heat of the day or the violence of the storm, medicines and herbs, planks to build his lodges, fibres to weave his clothing, and beauty for his surroundings—they were, as a rule, associated with good people who had been transformed to trees, as a means of putting an end to torments they endured in human form,[28] or as a reward by the gods. Philemon and Baucis were changed to a linden and an oak tree as a reward for their faithful service as Zeus's priests. Smyrna, mother of Adonis, was transformed by Aphrodite into a myrrh-tree to prevent her being killed by her father, King Cinyras. The drops of gum that flow from the bark are the tears Smyrna shed. Daphne, a beautiful mountain-nymph, was changed into a laurel-tree by Mother Earth so that she might escape the clutches of the amorous Apollo. These are but a few of the examples from Greek legend of the

28. There were a few exceptions to this general principle. According to a legend of the Haida Indians, the cedar trees on Queen Charlotte Island were once wicked people who constantly fought with each other, destroying the peace and happiness given to them at the creation. Similarly, in the Glooscap legends of the east coast, the old gnarled cedar tree came into being when Glooscap granted the wish of a visitor who asked for a long life. In this form, the visitor lived to an old age, indeed.

metamorphoses of humans to trees. Stories of a similar nature are found in the Indian legends.


## The Cathedral Trees of Stanley Park

In the heart of Stanley Park, Vancouver, huge fir trees form a vaulted dome, unmatched in beauty by any cathedral fashioned by the hand of man. The subdued light that filters through their branches and the hush that pervades the forest suggest that the spirit of the Creator lingers over his handiwork. These trees, called the "Cathedral trees of Stanley Park", are the inspiration for an Indian legend.

Long ago, an evil witch haunted the region of our western coast. Like Medusa of Greek legend, who transformed to stone everything upon which she cast her baleful eyes, all life that came within reach of this witch-woman's evil eye withered and died. In her company, dread Disease stalked the land and pale Famine lingered over the Indian villages; berries and fruit withered on the branch, and abundant catches of salmon were but memories of a happy past.

Then the Great Spirit, the Sagalie Tyee, resolved that if his creation, Man, were to survive, he must take action. To kill the witch-woman would not serve his purpose; her evil soul would live on. Therefore he summoned the four giants whom he used always to perform his work, and ordered them to turn the witch-woman into stone.

The four giants eagerly departed in their stone canoe. As they neared Prospect Point, they caught sight of the witch-woman. With a shrill laugh, she challenged them to do their worst. Then she fled into the depths of the forest (in what is now Stanley Park). Hurriedly beaching their canoe, the giants pursued

her, each covering hundreds of yards at a single stride of his huge legs. In the heart of the forest, they captured her. Then the mightiest of the giants raised his huge arm and uttered these words:

"Since you destroy everything that comes within your grasp, changing the bountiful life of our woods and rivers into barren emptiness, you shall be changed to stone, which harbours no life within its dry surface and which even the moss and vine will shun."

Whereupon the witch-woman was immediately transformed into a huge stone.

The Indians believe that, since her evil soul could not be destroyed, it lives on, locked within this rock. As evil has a magnetic attraction for those who come within its range, so those who penetrate to the heart of Stanley Park can never break free from the spell cast by this evil stone. Forever and ever, their spirits are doomed to circle this huge rock whose surface is covered with black stains, each stain standing for one of the witch-woman's evil deeds.

Knowing that Evil can be overcome only by Good, the Sagalie Tyee decided to place at the entrance to the trail something so great and good that men could withstand the lure of Evil. He chose from among his people the kindest and most unselfish, whose souls were filled with love for their fellow-beings. These he transformed into the tall, stately trees whose branches form an arch for his cathedral.


## Sequoyah and the Talking Leaves

The following story is not a legend, in the generally accepted definition of the word, because it deals with events that actually took place. It is, however, a story of courage and perseverance in the face of over-whelming difficulties; of considerable accomplishment after a lifetime of devotion to a cause; and of a quest, like that of the heroes of old, that ended in death.

The gigantic conifers of California (the big trees [*Sequoiadendron giganteum*] and the redwoods [*Sequoia sempervirens*]) are a source of wonder to all who behold them. A thousand years before the white man set foot on the North American Continent, many of these magnificent trees had reached full growth.

The *Sequoiadendron giganteum* and the *Sequoia sempervirens* are living testimony to the achievements of a Cherokee half-breed named Sequoyah. Some biographers refer to Sequoyah (the "Lame One") as an "untutored savage", although he provided his people, the Cherokee, with an alphabet—a method of communicating their language on paper, which the Indians called the "talking leaves" of the white man. Captain John Stewart in *A Sketch of the Cherokee and Choctow Indians* includes one of the first contemporary records of Sequoyah:

> His mother was a full-blooded Cherokee; and he was raised entirely among the uncultivated portion of the Cherokees, and never received much if any advantage from an intercourse with whites. He does not speak one word of the English language.[29]

Sequoyah may, or may not, have been a completely illiterate man. He became, however, a skilled craftsman and silversmith whose reputation for superb and delicate workmanship was known to the whites as well as to his own people. He was chosen to represent

29. Grant Foreman, *Sequoyah*

his people in their negotiations with the whites on at least two occasions.[30]

The motives that prompted Sequoyah to embark on a course that necessitated years of self-denial, alienated him from his wife, and, for a time, lost him the respect of his tribesman, are obscure. One explanation is that, during the War of 1812-14, he became fascinated by the "talking leaves" by means of which a soldier, simply by placing strange marks on a thin sheet of paper, fragile as the leaves that are swept into motion by a slight breath of wind, could send his voice thousands of miles away.

Another explanation is that he was prompted to consider writing in the Cherokee language in order to refute the idea, prevalent amongst the Cherokees, that the ability to put a talk on paper and send it any distance was an art far beyond the reach of an Indian. Still another explanation is that his interest was stimulated during the War when he discovered a letter in the possession of a captive.

Whatever awakened his interest in the "talking leaves", Sequoyah dreamed a dream which, like Deganoweda's vision of the great spruce tree, was to be an elusive light gleaming in the distance.[31] He beheld a vision of the day when his people, the Cherokees, would have discovered the secret of the "talking leaves"; when, able to communicate in their own language, they could send *their* words to others

30. He was a representative to the council called by Andrew Jackson which ceded 1,300,000 acres of Cherokee land in Tennessee to the United States. In 1828, he was one of the delegation of Western Cherokees who formed the treaty whereby their lands in Arkansas were exchanged for an extensive tract in what is now Oklahoma.
31. Deganoweda's vision of the spruce tree appears in the story "Hiawatha and Atotarho". See pages 183-191 of this book.

thousands of miles away or put them in books so that they could speak to their children and grandchildren.

Sequoyah's dream so dominated his life that he neglected both his trade as a silversmith and the upkeep of his house and farm. He devoted himself to the task of recording on birchbark every sound of the complex Cherokee speech. At first, despite herculean efforts, his endeavour met with failure. He recorded the sounds, but then forgot what his symbols represented. Derided by his wife, who finally became so infuriated with his neglect of practical concerns that she destroyed his manuscripts, and looked upon with scorn by his tribesmen, Sequoyah left home and lived the life of a recluse in an abandoned shack in the forest. Here he continued his laborious task. Only his ten-year-old daughter, Ah-yoka, retained her faith in him.

As night must yield to dawn and winter to spring, so in the face of his persistence, obstacles that at first appeared insurmountable were overcome. Conceiving the idea that the word should be divided into parts, or syllables, he made use of the white man's symbols to represent the syllables of Cherokee speech. Listening to speeches and conversation, he made a character for each distinctive syllable. At first, his alphabet consisted of an unwieldy 200 characters. These he gradually reduced to eighty-six.

Sequoyah had not only accomplished, but exceeded, his goal: the alphabet he developed was superior to the white man's in that the characters represented the same sound and there could be no errors in spelling. However success evaded him—for of what use was an alphabet if no one recognized it? Sequoyah was still looked upon as a dreamer!

Many of the Cherokees, in order to escape the white

man's persecution, had journeyed westward to Arkansas, where land had been promised to them "for as long as the grass grows or the water runs". They were no longer one nation but two, separated by a vast tract of wilderness. Sequoyah, who had joined the western migration, succeeded in arousing the interest of a few of his people in his written language when he took a letter from one of his pupils back to relatives in the east. When he read the letter to an astounded audience, some people, including Colonel Lowry, the Indian agent, realized that Sequoyah was not the dreamer they had thought him to be.

Success came in a dramatic manner when his alphabet was put to the test by the council of the Cherokees. Members of the council dictated what Sequoyah should write. Then his daughter Ah-yoka was summoned into the room and asked to read what had been written down. Before hushed and tense listeners, in a clear, confident voice, she read the words, just as they had been dictated.

The mystery of the "talking leaves" was revealed to the Cherokees, and Sequoyah's alphabet was put into immediate use. So simple was his system that an apt student could learn to read and write in one or two weeks. Within a few years, letters were pouring back and forth between the Cherokees who had set up new homes in the west and those who had remained in the east. The Cherokees achieved the distinction of becoming literate in a shorter period of time than any other race of people in history.

In 1835, those Cherokees who had remained in the east were forcibly removed from their homes and the long, disastrous western trek, aptly named the "Trial of Tears", began. In this expulsion, 4,000 people—mostly children and old folks—perished.

Meanwhile, rewards and praise had been heaped upon Sequoyah. His invention had done much to span the vast distance separating the eastern and western segments of his people. When the arrival of the "Treaty Party", as the newcomers were called, led to conflict with the older Cherokee settlers, Sequoyah did much to reconcile the two groups.

Sequoyah might have been expected to slip contentedly into quiet old age. But, just as Hiawatha, once he had accomplished his initial goal of uniting the Five Nations into the Iroquois Confederacy, devoted the remainder of his life to the task of uniting all the North American tribes into one confederation, so Sequoyah, by means of the "talking leaves", felt himself compelled to extend his good work. If he could invent an alphabet to record the Cherokee speech, thereby making his people one people, why could he not create a common alphabet for the diverse Indian tribes—an alphabet by means of which all tribes in North America could be united?

Hearing of a tribe in Mexico which was believed to be the origin of the Cherokees and hoping that their language would provide a common key to link together all the Indian languages, Sequoyah, at the age of seventy-two, set out with a small party on the long overland journey, through the southwestern states and on into Mexico.

However his body, weakened by age and hardship, was unable to fulfil the demands of his courageous spirit, and death ended his final quest. In an unmarked grave near the little town of San Fernando, Mexico, his body was returned to the earth whence it was formed.

Although many honours were heaped upon Sequoyah, to the Cherokees, the greatest testimony lies in the fact that his name will endure for as long as those wonders of the world of nature, the *Sequoia-dendron giganteum* and the *Sequoia sempervirens* stand. To this day, when the wind stirs the topmost branches of these trees, the Cherokees say that they are speaking of the past glories of the Indian people, and in particular of the bravest of the brave and the wisest of the wise—Sequoyah.

# 4
## *All Things Both Great and Small*

In the Book of Job, the Lord asked Job to behold the power of Leviathan as contrasted to the puniness of man:

> "The sword of him that layeth at him cannot hold: the spear, the dart, nor the habergeon.
> He esteemeth iron as straw, and brass as rotten wood.
> Darts are counted as stubble: he laugheth at the shaking of a spear . . .
> He maketh the deep to boil like a pot: he maketh the sea like a pot of ointment . . .
> He beholdeth all high things: he is a king over all the children of pride."

At this point, Job realized his own lowliness before the power of Him who had created Leviathan:

> But now my eye seeth thee. Wherefore I abhor myself and repent in dust and ashes.

Until comparatively recent times, this view of the animal world as a manifestation of the power of God prevailed. William Blake spoke of the "immortal hand or eye" that framed the "fearful symmetry" of the tiger. In Coleridge's ballad, the ancient mariner's sin drops from his neck when he blesses unawares the lowly organisms dwelling in the sea:

> He prayeth best who loveth best
> All things both great and small,
> For the dear God who loveth us
> He made and loveth all.

Charles Darwin in *On the Origin of Species by Means of Natural Selection* speaks of "the endless forms most beautiful and most wonderful that are being created from so simple a beginning".

However, from earliest times, a counter opinion of man's relationship with the animal world has existed: man has exalted himself to the role of master of the universe. The Bible refers to man as having been given "dominion over the fish of the sea, and over the fowl of the air, and over the cattle, and over all the earth"; for man, with his ability to reason, was made in the image of God. Shakespeare frequently exalts man's godlike reason and calls him "the paragon of the animals". Man's reason has enabled him to span continents, to subdue and tame beasts endowed with physical powers far exceeding his, and even to venture beyond this world in the conquest of outer space. Paradoxically, for the most of his advances there have been regressions. With gunpowder, man provided himself with a more efficient means of killing off his own kind and of extirpating entire species of wildlife. Atomic power, which should have been the open sesame to a brave new world of scientific progress, has become a Pandora's box unleashing the power that may result in man's extinction. Technological progress has polluted the very air man breathes and provided him with still another means of self-destruction.

Indeed, the time has come when we, like Job, shall "repent in dust and ashes" on beholding Leviathan, a testimony to a power, greater than ours, that shaped the universe. With humility, we should consider early man and examine his relationship with the animal world about him.

> Perhaps this life of ours, which begins as a quest of the child for the man, and ends as a journey by the man to rediscover the child, needs a clear image of some child-man.
>
> Laurens van der Post, *The Lost World of the Kalahari*

The child-man of whom van der Post was in quest was the African bushman. Before he succeeded in discovering the few remnants of this race, van der Post had gained some insight into their character through their surviving rock-painting.

> He never killed for fun or the sake of killing, and even when doing it was curiously apprehensive and regretful of the deed. The proof of all this is there in his paintings on his beloved rock for those who can see with their hearts as well as their eyes. There the animals of Africa still live as he knew them and as no European or Bantu artist has yet been able to render them. They are there not as quarry for his idle bow or food for his stomach, but as companions in mystery, as fellow pilgrims travelling on the same perilous spoor between distant life-giving waters.
>
> *Ibid.*

Though the North American Indian, too, has left us information about the past through rock-paintings,

the most vivid evidences of his relationship with the
animal world are carvings—particularly those revealed
in the Haida, Tlingit, and other highly structured
west-coast societies. The totem was the clan to which
an Indian belonged: these clans might originate from
supernatural animals, from whom the Indians traced
their descent or from whom their ancestors had experienced a supernatural revelation. Sometimes the
totem was derived from such animals as the killer
whale, raven, eagle, bear, beaver, or wolf, whom they
held in awe because of their power or cunning.[1]

> He cuts forms to fit the thoughts that the birds and
> animals and fish suggested to him, and to these he
> added something of himself. When they were all
> linked together they made very strong talk for the
> people. He grafted this new language on to the great
> cedar trunks and called them totem poles and stuck
> them up in the villages with great ceremony. Then the
> cedar and the creatures and the man all talked
> together through the totem poles to the people. The
> carver did even more—he let his imaginings rise above
> the objects that he saw and pictured supernatural
> beings too.
>
> The creatures that had flesh and blood like
> themselves the Indians understood. They accepted
> them as their ancestors but the supernatural things
> they feared and tried to propitiate.
>
> Then the missionaries came and took the Indians

1. For example, the bear clan originated from a Haida woman
   who was captured and taken prisoner by the king of bears, by
   whom she had a child half-human and half-bear. Romans and
   Greeks also traced their origin to animals; e.g. Romulus and
   Remus who were nursed by a wolf and Zeus, king of the gods,
   who was nursed by the she-goat, Amalthea. The carvings are
   relatively new since they began only after the coming of iron
   tools. The clans had long been established by this time.

away from their old villages and the totem poles and
put them into new places where life was easier, where
they bought things from a store instead of taking
them from nature.

Emily Carr, *Klee Wyck*

Primitive man reverenced power, whether in the
natural phenomena that could wipe out entire
communities at a blow, or in animals whose strength
so exceeded his as to make his mightiest efforts futile.
The early Egyptians respected and revered the bird,
with its power of flight; the lion, with its immense
strength; the crocodile, which lurked in the river mud
and could take off a man's leg with a snap of its jaws;
the snake, with its furtive motion; and the ibis, with
its air of wisdom. In time, the high-flying falcon
became one of the insignia of royalty; the crocodile,
the infernal monster which devoured guilty souls. The
ibis became Thoth, the god of wisdom; and the lion,
like the sphinx, symbolized kingly majesty.[2]

This reverence for the (apparent) superiority of
animals is reflected throughout Greek mythology. The
first evidence of it is seen in the story of creation.
Epimetheus, He Who Thinks Afterwards, created the
animals before man. He gave them strength, speed,
and cunning, sharp claws and sharp teeth, and
protective robes of feathers and fur. Nothing
remained for man—his puny, shivering last creation.
It was left for Prometheus, He Who Thinks Ahead, to
intervene on man's behalf and rectify, in part, the
error of his brother.[3]

Throughout the Golden Age, or the Age of
Innocence, man lived at peace with his fellow man

2. Leonard Cottrell, *Life Under the Pharaohs*, Pan Books
3. For the Greek version of the creation of man read Jay
   Macpherson, *The Four Ages of Man*.

and the animals of the forest. They, in turn, never troubled him. Then man began to build shelters and sow grain, and learned to harness the animals to his use. Nevertheless both legend and religious rites give ample testimony to the awe and mystery which prevailed in man's attitude towards the animal world. Often the animal was worshipped outright. This was true of the minotaur, half-bull and half-man, who dwelt in the underground labyrinth of King Minos's palace at Knossus.[4] As narrated in the story of Theseus, yearly sacrifices of seven youths and seven maidens were made to propitiate the minotaur.

Evidence of the original practice of worshipping animals occurs in myths where a god or goddess changes to an animal. Two sea deities, Thetis and Proteus, had the ability to transform themselves at will to lions, bears, or serpents. Pan, the god of shepherds, was part-goat and part-man. Zeus, who was nursed by the she-goat Amalthea in a remote cave in Mount Ida, often assumed the shape of an animal to conceal his illicit affairs from his ever-vigilant wife, Hera. Ares, the war god, changed himself into a wild boar in order to murder his rival, Adonis.

As man became aware of the goals which his reason made possible for him to attain, his worship of animal deities declined and eventually disappeared. A suggestion of this development may be seen in the stories in which men, not gods, were changed into animals. Indo-European legends tell of the prince who was changed into a wolf, a frog, or a bear, and restored to his human form by the touch of a beautiful maiden.

4. Minos himself was descended from a bull, being the offspring of Zeus and Europa. Zeus, according to his custom when enamoured of mortal woman, had assumed the form of a bull when he abducted Europa. See R.S. Lambert, "Theseus and the Minotaur", *Myths, Legends and Fables*.

Eventually, in sacrificial rites, animals were substituted for the human offering. For example, in the fertility rites where the king had formerly been sacrificed, because his body and blood were believed to have restorative powers, animals became the sacrificial victims.

Even after the animal has been relegated to the role of victim, the Greeks did not neglect to show it respect. When it was killed to be eaten, it was a sacrifice: its bones and inedible parts were offered to the gods.[5] Unwarranted slaughter of animals was condemned. Following the abduction of Helen, the Greeks, en route to Troy, were held up by hostile winds, and counsel was sought as to the reason for the gods' opposition. The explanation offered was that the Greeks had killed a stag sacred to Artemis. When Phrixus, in response to the will of the gods, sacrificed the golden ram which had carried him to safety, its fleece had to be accorded due respect. It was nailed to a tree in the War God's Wood. Even so, the spirit of Phrixus knew no rest until the fleece was restored to its rightful place in its country of origin.[6] This respect for the victim is shown in John Keats's beautiful recreation of the sacrificial scene:

Who are those coming to the sacrifice?
To what green altar, O mysterious priest,
Leadest thou that heifer lowing at the skies,
And all her silken flanks with garlands drest?
"On a Grecian Urn"

5. Hence, in the New Testament, there is the problem of meat being offered to idols. Orthodox Jews still require meat to be killed in the kosher manner.
6. See Edith Hamilton, "The Quest for the Golden Fleece", *Mythology*.

## The Apology for Death

After he had been persuaded by the conspirators that
the death of Caesar was necessary to the regeneration
of Rome, Brutus conveyed his feelings about the
assassination:

> Let us be sacrificers, but not butchers, Caius.
> Let's carve him as a dish fit for the gods,
> Not hew him as a carcass fit for hounds.
>> Shakespeare, *Julius Caesar*, II, i,166-68

Primitive man's attitude to the killing of the creatures
of the forests and oceans was essentially the same.
Killing was a necessity, not a pleasure. He regretted
taking the life of a noble being, one whose cunning,
strength, speed, and endurance far exceeded his and
who, therefore, merited worship, not desecration. For
this reason, the Indians have been sound conser-
vationists, killing only when it was essential and
accompanying the killing with rites befitting the
dignity and worth of the animal. Killing an animal was
a sacrifice, and if the ceremony were performed in an
appropriate manner, some of the animal's strength,
ferocity, and cunning would be passed on to those
partaking of its flesh. These ceremonies, performed
by Indians and Eskimos throughout all parts of what
is now Canada, have been termed by anthropologists
"the apology for death".

### 1 The Hunting of the White Whale

Prior to the hunt, the captain, i.e., the man who actually threw the harpoon, had to withdraw from the
people. Going to a building where the skulls of former
harpooners looked down upon him, he prayed for
success, and abstained from eating or from doing

anything that might displease the spirits of the whales. He purified himself by bathing in the cold, crystal-clear waters of a lake far removed from the village where his people dwelt, and purged himself further by rubbing his body with bundles of hemlock twigs until the blood came. In like manner, all the members of the crew had to cleanse and purify themselves in readiness for the sacrifice. Among the Unalit, any hunter who has had a hand in the killing of a white whale, or even has helped to take one from the net, is not allowed to do any work for the next four days, that being the time during which the spirit of the whale is supposed to stay with its body.[7]

When the dead animal was towed back to the village and drawn up on the beach, the people sang songs of welcome, thanking him for coming to their home, and praising him for his size. Then the body was cut up in proportions determined by ceremonial rules, the most honourable piece being the one between the head and the dorsal fin. While the remainder was apportioned to the people, this piece was put on a framework and decorated with feathers.

7. J.G. Frazer, *The Golden Bough*

Thus the spirit of the great white whale, having been duly honoured, was appeased and the people could now partake of his body.

*2 Salmon Rites*

The first "Salmon Ceremony" of the Kwakiutl tribe inhabiting the coastal regions of what is now British Columbia was similar to the rites of the whale-hunters. The purpose of the ceremony was also the same; to propitiate the spirit of the salmon and to greet the salmon's arrival at their village. This ritual was undertaken as soon as the first catch was obtained from an important stream in an area where the fishing camp was located. The priest, or shaman officiating, addressed the salmon as though it were a chief of high rank visiting them; usually, he presented it with an offering. Then the fish was cooked and its body broken and distributed to all those participating in the ceremony. The ritual having been concluded with the eating of the fish, the whole tribe was now free to engage in fishing for its livelihood.[8]

The result of the needless slaughtering of the forest creatures is illustrated in a story from our northwest coast. Living in a land overflowing with an abundance of animal and fish life, the younger people forgot the traditions of their ancestors and wantonly killed small animals, leaving their carcasses to rot in the fields. The horrified elders warned these foolish youths that, though the Sky Chief approved of killing for food, vengeance from the spirit world would be wreaked on those who persisted in needless slaughter.

But the young people scoffed at the fears of their elders. One day, when the salmon run was at its

8. E.S. Rogers, "The Kwakiutl". *The Beaver*, spring issue, 1969

height, with myriads of salmon crowding up the rivers to spawn, these young men, to satisfy their craving for excitement, caught many salmon, made slits in the fishes' backs, inserted pieces of burning pitch pine, and put them back into the river so that the salmon swam about in the water like living torches. Indifferent to the suffering of the fish, the cruel youngsters laughed as they watched the intricate patterns of the flames traced against the darkness of the river.

Eventually the day of reckoning arrived. One evening, after the salmon run was over and winter was drawing near, a rumbling noise like the far-off beating of medicine drums could be distinguished. Each night, the mysterious sounds drew closer. An ominous presence seemed to hang over the land. Now, even the young people were fearful.

Then the beating grew loud as thunder; the mountains burst open and rivers of moving fire gushed towards the village. Panic-stricken, the people plunged into the forests hoping to escape, but few were able to do so. By now, the forests were a flaming holocaust. True to the predictions of their elders, the spirit world had wreaked vengeance on those responsible for the suffering of the salmon.

*3 The Beaver Rites of the Chipewyan and Ojibway Indians*
The animal that provided the main sustenance of each tribe was revered and glorified as the giver and sustainer of life. The Indians on the plains held the buffalo in special veneration, while the Indians of the northern forest areas, particularly the Chipewyan and Ojibway, worshipped the beaver because it was a source of both meat and clothing. As the following legend illustrates, the Chipewyan believe that their race owes its origin to the beaver.

When the world was young, animals were larger, more intelligent, and more powerful than they are today; consequently, they ruled over men, who were their slaves. As the race of men grew more intelligent, they revolted against the domination of the beaver, who was forced to fly from his beaver lodge at Lake Athabaska. Badly wounded, the animal dived under-water. As he swam, he left a trail of blood in his wake. Reaching the far side, he climbed up the rocky shore. Here he died. His blood dripping on the rocks stained them a deep red which has endured to this day. From

this same blood was brought to life the first Chipewyan race.

To this century, before killing a beaver, the Chipe-
wyans apologize to it for the necessity of doing so.

The Ojibway likewise show a proper reverence to
this animal that is their source of life, "carving him
as a dish fit for the gods, not hewing him as a carcass
fit for hounds". No Ojibway would ever throw the
bones of a beaver to the dogs. It is believed that a dog
bites harder than a human, and that a beaver feels it
when a dog chews his bones. All the bones are tied
in a bundle of clean cloth, together with ribbons and
tobacco, and thrown into the water where no dog can
get at them. The spirit of the beaver having been
properly propitiated, the Indian will enjoy good luck
in the coming season.

*4 Sacred Bear Beliefs*
It is not surprising to find special reverence accorded
to the bear from tribes ranging from the Ottawa, in
the east, to the Nootka and Tsimsyan of our western
coast. More than any other North American animal,
the bear possesses a striking physical resemblance to
man. It often stands or sits upright, its awkward
movements seeming to parody the clumsy efforts of
a man in a heavy coat two sizes too big for him. This
"poker face of the woods" often appears to engage in
conversation, its ears and head moving as if participating in heated controversy.

The Indians observed the man in the bear, or the
bear in the man. Hence, in the legends of many tribes,
the bear was at one time a human. If an Ojibway
meets a bear, he addresses it in fear as "our grandfather to all of us".[9] Nor should we scoff at this

9. Amongst the Ojibways of Parry Island are many stories of the
   bear-walker, a person who uses evil medicine to change

simplicity, for modern evolutionary theory is that we and the bear, our brother, are descended from a common ancestor.

The following Cree legend illustrates the link between the bear and the human.

## The Enchanted Bear

There once lived two sisters who lost their parents when the younger one was but a baby, and the older child about twelve years of age. The latter resolved to bring up her baby sister herself by providing for her food and clothing and in every possible way taking the place of their parents. To accomplish this task, she devoted her days to working for the women of the village, who gave her food in return for her help. Long hours she laboured, weaving strips of skins into sheets for clothing, scraping skins, sewing clothing, grinding corn, and preparing game for eating.

Occasionally, the sisters had to content themselves with soup, made from the bones of animals which the girl placed in a skin bag and immersed in a pot of water, heated by dropping hot stones into it. Usually, the village women, appreciative of her endeavours on behalf of her baby sister, were able to reward her efforts more adequately.

The girl placed on the younger sister only one restriction—that she never take part in the game "Bear". In this game, one child, pretending to be a bear, would pursue the other children as they fled, in mock alarm, in all directions until one was caught.

himself into a bear in order to wreak vengeance on an enemy. They are used to this day to frighten children into good behaviour, much as the bogey man is utilized by white mothers.

However the younger sister possessed the active nature of all normal healthy children. In spite of her resolution to obey her sister, one day she yielded to temptation and joined in the game. Other than the pangs of conscience that one would expect, she enjoyed herself thoroughly and was relieved to find that nothing unpleasant happened to her as a result of her disobedience. Nothing unusual occurred, that is, until she returned home. Then, to her dismay, she discovered that her sister had turned into a bear.

Heartbroken, she accompanied her bear-sister to a cave near the river.

The younger sister now became a subject of ridicule. People mocked her because her sister was a bear. On one occasion, heedless of the fact that they were in the vicinity of the cave, they taunted the poor girl. Suddenly, out rushed the bear, killing the nearest of her tormentors with one blow of her paw.

After this, the villagers kept a watchful eye on the cave and waylaid the young girl, holding her captive until she told them where the bear kept her heart. Not realizing that any harm would come of it, she divulged the secret: her bear-sister kept her heart in the little toe of her forepaw.

That night the Indians drove sticks, pointed at both ends, into the ground surrounding the cave. The next morning they stood outside the cave shouting abuse and ridicule at the bear. Finally, in a frenzy of rage, she rushed from the cave, whereupon her forepaw was pierced by one of the stakes.

Heedless of her own safety, the younger sister ran from the cave to the aid of her sister, who had fallen to the ground. It was too late—she was dead.

The Indians believed the bear's bones were sacred and used them for charms and relics for sucking rites.

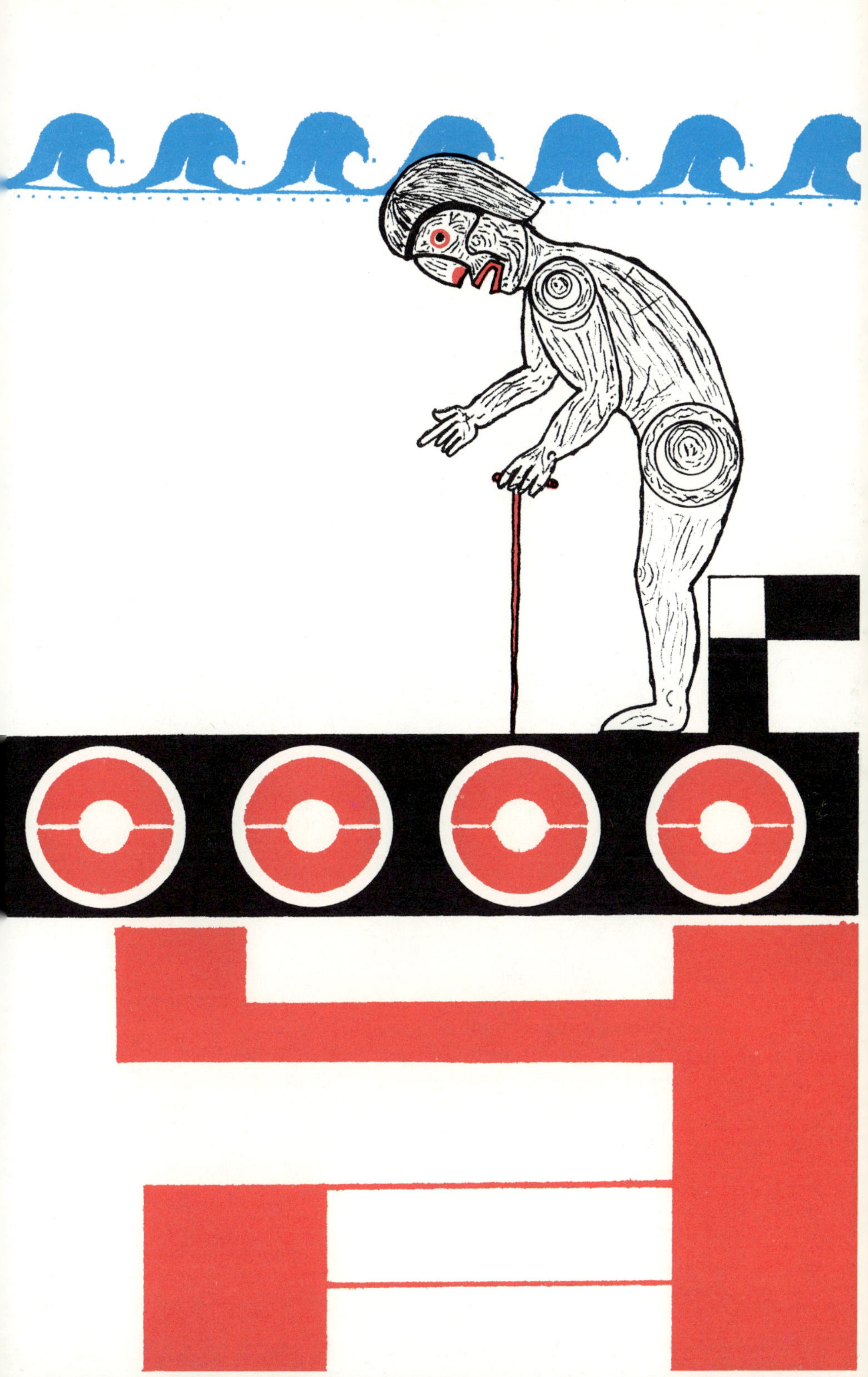

Hollow bones from the legs or arms were used to suck out disease or sickness brought on by sorcery. The front teeth were made into whistles and charms.

J.G. Frazer gives a vivid description of the ceremony performed by the Nootka Indians when a bear had been killed:

> The dead bear was brought in and seated before the
> head chief in an upright posture, with a chief's
> bonnet, wrought in figures, on its head, and its fur
> powdered over with white down. A tray of provisions
> was then set before it, and it was invited by words and
> gestures to eat. After that the animal was skinned,
> boiled, and eaten.
>
> J.G. Frazer, *The Golden Bough*

Animal legends taken from Greek and Indian cycles have a common source: the recognition of the *oneness* of life. They refer to a time when the world was without secrets between one form of being and another, "to the moment which our European fairy-tale books described as the time when birds, beasts, plants, trees, and men shared a common tongue, and the whole world, night and day, resounded like the surf of a coral sea with universal conversation."[10]

## *Birds*

> Do you think that I have less divination than the
> swans? For they, when they knew that they must die,
> having sung all their lives sing louder than ever, for
> joy at going home to the god that they serve. Men,
> who themselves fear death, have taken it for
> lamentation, forgetting no bird sings in hunger, or

10. Laurens van der Post, *The Lost World of the Kalahari*

cold, or pain. But being Apollo's children, they share his gift of prophecy, and foresee the joys of another world.

Plato, Phaedo

The above excerpt refers to the legend of the swan who, having a premonition of his death, drifts to a secluded section of the stream, the surrounding hills and valleys echoing and re-echoing to the dying cadence of his lamentations.

Birds have a special place in the legendary hierarchy of the animal world. Not only are they endowed with grace of motion and with plumage rivalling the rainbow, but also with the power to venture into the realm of the gods themselves.

In Greek legend, the swan has been especially favoured. Its snow-white plumage, its grace and dignity, and the V-shape of its flying formation (a female symbol) account for its predominant role. Zeus assumed the shape of a swan when visiting Leda, the mother of Helen of Troy. Apollo chose the swan form for his son Cycnus,[11] when he leaped into the lake after having been confronted by Phylius.

As a subject for many of their legends, the Indians have chosen the loon. Its melancholy cry reverberating from the rocks and crags of our remote northern lakes held the same haunting appeal for the Indians as did the lament of the dying swan for the early Greeks. Another source of mystery associated with the loon was its ability to swim, faster than any fish, as far as 150 feet under the surface of the water. For this reason, the loons, in most Indian legends, were the messengers of the gods. The following legend is perhaps the best known.

11. Hence the word *cygnet* for the offspring of the swan

## The Loon's Necklace

### A Legend of the Interior Salish

In the Indian village of Shulus, on the banks of the
Nicola River, there lived long ago an old blind
medicine man, named Kelora. Because of his
blindness, he was miserably poor, hardly able to
support himself and his wife.

Though he called himself a medicine man, he really
did little but dream. In the summer he would sit all
day long in the shade of the trees and in winter he
would sun himself with his back propped against the
house, wrapped in a tattered blanket of groundhog
skins to keep out the cold. Now and then his wife
would scold him for his idleness.

"After all," she would remind him, "you're not the
only blind man there is. Look at Intameen, up there
near Quilchena. He finds plenty to do. He gets the
spruce roots ready for his wife when she makes
baskets, and he makes the most beautiful bone beads,
and even spins the twine to thread them on. And all
you do is sit here grinning at the sun, and scratching
your worthless old hide."

Only once had he tried to excuse himself and
remind her that he was, after all, a medicine man and,
he would have liked to add, should be shown some
respect. Were not medicine men important people?

"A medicine man! You, a medicine man? Nobody
ever comes to you unless every other healer he has
heard of has failed. 'Fast four days,' you tell
everybody the same thing. 'Then take four sweat
baths, still fasting, and then chew four juniper berries,
taking care to swallow all the juice.' It's four of this,
and four of that! Rubbish! Any nitwit could give the
same advice and get more for the giving of it."

Old Kelora didn't seem to mind at all. He just sat
staring up at the sun as though he had not heard a

word of what she had said. There was only one sound that was sure to rouse him and that was the cry of the loon, the strangest and, perhaps, the most lovely of all woodland sounds. Whenever he heard it, a great restlessness seemed to seize him. His blind hands would fumble for his stick and then he would start off, groping his way along the little trail beside the creek that flows out of Mamette Lake. Slowly and painfully he would go, his stick feeling the way, and an upraised elbow shielding his eyes from the twigs and branches that hung over the trail.

Sometimes he was gone for days and, when he returned, tired out, half starved, stained with mud where he had stumbled on the way, he would say nothing of where he had been.

"I have been talking with my father, the Loon," he would explain patiently, and that was all.

After a long wet autumn, it happened that there was a very poor crop of the berries the Indians used to dry for their winter food, and then a very hard, cold season began. Every day the men came home to the village from their hunting with almost no game. There seemed to be no deer, no grouse, no rabbits, but the tracks of wolves were everywhere in the snow. With so little fresh meat, the people were forced to use up their stocks of dried food, and the thousands of salmon which they had smoked during the summer were being eaten much too fast.

The older men met together and wondered whether they should send some young men to nearby villages and even as far away as Kamloops and Lytton, to Tulameen, and even to Lillooet to try to buy food.

One day, after the hunters had come home again empty-handed, old Kelora spoke to the chief.

"Tell your young men and the hunters to be on their guard," he said. "The wolves are hungry too, just as we are, for they have killed all the game in the valley. Soon they will come right into the village and try to steal the children."

The chief, worried and anxious, turned away from
the old blind man.

"Go back to your dreaming," he laughed. "I have no
time for the chatter of fools. Go back to your medicine
making and listen for the call of the loon."

Now hardly a full day had passed, when the women
were startled to hear the scream of a child. Running
down to the river bank, they caught sight of a large
gray wolf, trotting easily towards Warm Springs.
They found some blood stains on the snow, a little
winter cap of squirrel skins, a toy bow, the tracks of
a child,—and of the wolf.

"Old Kelora was right," said the chief. "Even the
wolves are starving now."

The wolves grew bolder and bolder. Grown men
were no longer safe alone, but had to hunt in pairs.
Traps were set and deadfalls built; many wolves were
killed, but their numbers hardly seemed to grow less.
The people were becoming very much afraid and
there was even talk of abandoning the whole village of
Shulus and moving somewhere else, an almost
unheard of thing to do, especially in the dead of
winter.

Old Kelora said this would not be wise, and this
time the chief listened to him.

"Do you think we could move more quickly than
the wolves could follow us?" he asked, and he was
quite plainly right.

"True," the people admitted, "but what are we to
do? We are starving, and our children are starving
with us."

Old Kelora knew now that the time for which he
had waited so long had come at last. If the village
could be saved at all, it would be by Kelora's use of
his own powers of magic. When he was a boy he had
spent many days all alone on the far hilltops, bathing
in little lakes, scrubbing himself with harsh hemlock

JASON BEEHI '72

twigs till the blood flowed, starving himself for days on end that he might become a medicine man.

He had not gone through all these hardships for nothing, for in every one of his visions the Loon had appeared to him, and given him powers not known to other men. Nobody had ever guessed that Kelora really had magical powers for he had never proved it to anybody, not even to the most powerful chiefs or important medicine men. Only when there was some serious danger would his guardian spirit allow the singing of his sacred songs, the wearing of his collar of gleaming white dentalium shells, each shaped like a tiny elephant's tusk, or the use of his magical bow. But now, he knew, the right time had come to use the powers that had been given him.

Carefully he felt his way down to the frozen river's edge where the village sweat houses stood on the sandy bank. Four times he steamed himself in the sweat house and four times he plunged into the ice-cold river. Then he made his way home, put on his sacred collar of dentalium shells, and sang aloud his mystical songs. He strung his magical bow and picked out four arrows with their sharp stone tips.

Hardly had he finished getting ready when he heard a shout. Once more the wolves were coming right into the village, hoping to steal some uncared-for child.

In strong, clear tones, Old Kelora told his wife to lead him quickly towards the wolves. She was so surprised that she obeyed without thinking. As soon as they appeared in the village street there were shouts of laughter.

"Are you going to throw him to the wolves?" they asked. "Take him back home. What does he know about shooting wolves?"

"Pay no attention to them," Kelora ordered her, "but point my arrow towards the biggest wolf. Carefully now. As though you yourself were going to shoot."

"All right. Up a little," she said. "A bit more to this side. So. Now. Let fly your arrow."

Old Kelora let fly. Swift and true went the arrow, straight to the flank of a huge wolf hiding in a little patch of brush.

"Look! Look!" cried the people who had been watching. "What a shot! No ordinary man could shoot like that even if he could see properly. Kelora must be a magician. A great magician. We shall all be saved, thanks to Kelora the magician."

The old man said nothing, but turned back to his home.

For the rest of the winter, whenever the wolves were seen he would go out to the edge of the village. Always he made his wife get his aim straight, and always he killed the wolf he shot at. At last they drew off, looking for safer hunting grounds, and once more the village hunters were able to bring back game.

During the next summer, Old Kelora decided to go once more to visit his guardian spirit, the Loon. He walked for miles in the distant hills till the day was nearly done. He paused in thought and then he felt the warmth of the setting sun on his left cheek.

"So," he murmured to himself, "then the little lake I once knew so well should lie right ahead of me, just a little way over the top of the sloping ground."

Suddenly, as if to prove that he was right, he heard the long-drawn, quavering cry of the Loon.

Slowly and cautiously he made his way forward, his feet tripped by roots, his face scatched by the underbrush. At last, as the sun sank lower, the rank lush smell of the lake grew strong and he heard the plop of a frog as it jumped into the water. Soon he felt the damp earth sink slightly beneath his moccasins and, bending down, he touched with his finger tips the cool, still water.

Kelora drew himself to his full height as he stood facing the lake, his own lake as he always called it. He lifted his hand to his throat to make sure he still had his sacred collar of dentalium shells, and he sang once more the sacred songs he had learned near this very spot so long ago. Then he called aloud.

"Oh, my Father, the Loon," he cried. "Come to me now. Help me, my Father."

Close by his feet, a voice answered him.

"What is it that my son desires?"

"I am blind, my Father, and I wish to see."

"Climb then upon my back," said the Loon.

Awkwardly Kelora seated himself on the bird's back.

"Now, clasp me tightly and hold your breath," cried the Loon and he dived deep into the waters of the lake and swam swiftly and strongly to the other side.

"Can you see now, my son?" he asked.

"I see, but not as a man should see, for there is still a thick fog over my eyes."

"Hold tight once more," cried the Loon, and again they plunged deep into the water. Four times in all they swam below the surface from side to side of the lake.

"Now I see! I see, and it is as if I had never known blindness!" cried Kelora.

He turned to give thanks to the one who had made him see again, but there was nobody there at all, just a loon swimming quietly on the still water.

None but the dearest of all his treasures would be enough. Old Kelora took off the collar of little white shells and, with a wide sweep of his arm, tossed it gently towards the loon.

Spinning slowly as it sailed through the air, the collar wrapped itself round the bird's throat, making the shining white necklace we see there today.

A handful of shells, which broke away from the string, fell scattered on the loon's back.

These, too, you may see on any loon.

*Dr. Douglas Leechman*

## Wesukechak and the Loon

Not all Indians thought of the loon as a beautiful and graceful creature. The Crees, in particular, were struck by the ludicrous and grotesque in its appearance and actions. They noted its stubby tail and the legs attached far back on the body which caused it to move awkwardly on land by pushing along on its breast in frog-like leaps. Its cries, rising from the loneliness of the lake, seemed to them a weird howling. The story of Wesukechak and the Loon is an attempt to account for the peculiarities of this strange bird. Like most legends, it reveals much of the character of the people who created it.

It is said that man made the gods in his own image. We have seen that this is true of the Greeks, whose gods possessed such human traits as lust, jealousy, and envy. Wesukechak, the god of the Crees, also reflected human qualities. As a god, he was powerful enough to have created the sun, the moon, and the stars; to have remade the earth after the Flood; and to have peopled it with all living things. As a man, he was kind to his children. When the birds grew tired of their drab colours, he produced a quantity of paints rivalling the rainbow in variety. With these, he painted the birds the colours they requested. He it was who gave the animals their handsome, warm coats. In some respects, Wesukechak was only too human. Many of the stories about him depict his overwhelming curiosity and his tendency to interfere in other people's business. This often involved him in humiliating situations. Like the Greek gods Hermes and Pan, and like Napi of the Blackfoot, Crow of the Kutchin, Raven of the west-coast tribes, Coyote of the western plateau, and other Indian gods or demigods,

Wesukechak was a trickster and often ended up the victim of his own pranks.

The Crees never tired of listening to stories of Wesukechak and the animals, and it is said that he who tells all the stories of Wesukechak is assured a long life. Their delight in these stories illustrates not only their whimsical sense of humour but also their feeling of identity with the world of nature around them.

One evening, just as dusk cast its shadow on the land, Wesukechak heard the honking of geese. At this familiar sound of spring, his heart was glad, for winter had been long and hard; neither his snares nor his bow and arrow had procured much game. Wesukechak was hungry. His spirits soared when he realized, as the sounds became louder and louder, that the huge flock was alighting on the marsh not far from his campsite.

Next morning he hurried to the marsh and feasted his eyes on the thousands of geese clamouring on its surface. His mouth watered as he thought of the delicious feast within his reach. He resolved to get as much food as possible by relying on trickery rather than on his bow and arrow.

He gathered a big bundle of muskeg moss and put it on his back. Then, walking, head bent, along the edge of the marsh, he pretended not to notice the geese until they spotted him and in their curiosity, cried out, "Wesukechak, Wesukechak, what have you there?"

"It's only a song bag," replied Wesukechak.

"Let us hear your songs, Wesukechak," begged the birds, fluttering their wings as they clambered to the shore.

"You should realize," answered Wesukechak, "that

I can't sing my songs until I have built a wigwam to sing in. If you really want to hear my songs, why don't you help me build my wigwam?"

Immediately the geese came to Wesukechak's assistance, and, while he cut stout saplings and thrust them into the ground, bending them into hoops to form the frame, they gathered strips of cedar bark and covered the frame. With spruce boughs, they covered the floor. Soon the huge wigwam was completed and Wesukechak invited the geese to enter and hear his songs. As they flocked inside, he smacked his lips in anticipation of the delicious feast that was soon to be his.

Joyfully, Wesukechak began singing, and the geese, catching his enthusiasm, kept time to the beat of his songs, following his instructions implicitly as he called them out. Only the loon, which kept near the entrance, did not share the joy of the occasion.

"For the next dance, you will lie down on the floor," cried Wesukechak, sensing that the time had come to spring his cunning trap.

Without question, thinking it was part of the next dance, the geese carried out his instructions.

"Now close your eyes and join me as I sing my song," called out Wesukechak. Immediately all the geese closed their eyes.

Wesukechak continued his singing, the birds joining him. But, as he sang, he thrust his hands out and wrung the necks of the geese nearest him.

So trusting were the geese that Wesukechak would have accomplished his plan and enjoyed the biggest feast of his life had it not been for the loon. Suspicious of Wesukechak from the start, he had kept one eye partially open. As soon as he saw what Wesukechak was up to, he cried out in alarm, "Wesukechak is going to kill us all. Run, run!"

The geese fluttered to the doorway, most of them making their escape in spite of the frenzied efforts of Wesukechak to stop them. In his rage, he kicked the loon just as it was taking flight.

Ever since, the loon has had a stubby tail and, to this day, limps about on land, which he avoids travelling on, if he can. He prefers the seclusion of the northern lakes, where he can be heard still howling in pain.

## Ceyx and Alcyone

Folded, impervious, at peace they rest
As though this lustrous treachery were their home.
And safely they could build far out. A nest
Would live for months, twisted from tufts of foam.

> Their breasts against the breathing of the deep
> Are blue clouds in a sky of constant weather.
> And so the sky on this ambiguous sleep
> Glides down, falls like a blue king-fisher's feather.
>> Douglas Le Pan, "Interval with Halcyons"

The legend of Ceyx and Alcyone is the Greek interpretation of the origin of the kingfisher, or halcyon, and an explanation of the seven days of calm preceding and following the winter solstice. During these fourteen days, sea and sky are one, as the placid surface of the Mediterranean Sea mirrors the blue heavens.

Alcyone, daughter of Aeolus, guardian of the winds, married Ceyx, the son of the Morning Star. The two were very much in love and their married life, blest by the Olympian gods, seemed destined to be long and happy. But, when mortals dwell in a state of paradise resembling the life of the gods, they tend to become presumptuous and think of themselves as gods. This was true of Alcyone, who incurred the wrath of cloud-gathering Zeus by comparing herself and Ceyx to Hera and Zeus. Great was the fury of Zeus! The earth trembled and the waters heaved as he hurled his mighty thunderbolts at the ship bearing Ceyx home from a journey he had made to consult the oracles. He was swept from the wreckage of the ship into the turbulent waves. The last words on his dying lips were, "Alcyone, Alcyone, my beloved wife."

All this was unknown to Alcyone, who eagerly awaited the return of her husband and the resumption of their idyllic life. As the days passed, eagerness gave way to anxiety. She offered prayers to the gods, above all, to Hera, protectress of married love, for Ceyx's return.

Resentful of her impetuous husband's interference,

Hera resolved to do what she could to relieve the anxiety gnawing at the heart of the unhappy Alcyone. Summoning her messenger, the rainbow goddess Iris, she bade her go to the house of Somnus, the god of Sleep, to ask that a dream be sent to Alcyone telling her the truth.

Now the home of Sleep lies in the land of the Cimmeronians, in a deep valley where the sun never shines, and all is clothed in the twilight world of shadows. The woodlands surrounding old Somnus's home are the realm of Sleep: there is no breeze to sway the branches of the black poplars into activity, and no birds sing. The hypnotic murmuring of the River Lethe, as it drifts towards the dark, underground caverns, lulls him deeper and deeper into slumber. Before his cave, hosts of drowsy poppies droop weary heads over slender stems. Inside, Somnus himself, in the farthest and darkest corner of the cave, reclines on a downy couch, black as Erebus.

To this half world, lying between the living and the dead, came Iris in her multihued robe. Entering the cave, she discerned Somnus drowsing on his couch. At first, she had difficulty in rousing him sufficiently to make Hera's command known to him. Then, in a voice still thick with sleep, he agreed to send his son Morpheus to Alcyone in a dream which would reveal to her the death of her husband.

That night Morpheus, the dream-god, assuming the form of her drowned husband, appeared to Alcyone. His wide eyes were bulging as if about to burst from their sockets in horror of dreadful death; his skin was the ashen hue of death. With water dripping from his soaking clothes, he leaned over her couch. "Poor Alcyone," he said. "I am here beside you. Is my face so changed by death that you do not know me? Never more will your lovely features look upon me in the land of the living. However cease not your weeping. Look for my body in Poseidon's watery kingdom, for, if it is not given proper burial rites, my soul must wait for a hundred years, beseeching entrance into Pluto's dark realm.''

With a start, Alcyone awoke and looked about her, but the form of Ceyx had vanished. She rushed down to the shore and gazed out to sea. In the dim light of early dawn, she saw an indistinct form floating on the surface of the water. Gradually the waves carried it closer and closer until she recognized it as Ceyx's body. With a wild cry of anguish, she leaped into the sea, her only thought being to join her husband in death.

As she plunged into the water, her body was borne aloft by the wind, and she felt herself being carried over the surface of the blue waves. The pitying gods had changed her into a kingfisher. She was soon joined by another kingfisher, Ceyx, who likewise had been transformed, and togther they swooped and skimmed over the surface of the Mediterranean.

Now, every winter, the male kingfisher dies and, with great wailing, his mate carries his dead body to his burial. Then, building a nest from thorns of the sea-needle, she launches it on the sea, lays her eggs, and broods over them until they are hatched. During the fourteen-day period, her father, Aeolus, keeps the winds locked in his cave in the Tyrrhenian Sea.[12] In memory of the beautiful Alcyone, we call the kingfishers ''halcyons'', and the fourteen days when the waters of the Mediterranean are mirror-still, as by magic, are referred to as the ''halcyon'' days.

In the legends of all nations, birds are depicted as messengers that usually bring good tidings to

12. Robert Graves, *The Greek Myths*: II

mankind. Their swift flight and cheerful notes account for this association. After all, angels have wings, and Hermes, the messenger of Zeus, was given winged sandals to speed him on his errands. The dove was depicted as a messenger, not only in Greek stories, but in the Book of Genesis as well. Long ago, the Indians conceived of the robin, with his bright breast, "cheer-up" song, and quick movements, as a harbinger of spring.

## The First Robin

Many, many years ago an old Ojibway named Grey Falcon was blessed with an only son long after his wife had passed the usual years of childbearing. The birth of a son in the declining years of the old man's life gave new hope and purpose to everything he did. He called the child Wahbi Ahmik, or White Beaver, in memory of a great leader of his people, and lived for the day when his son would perform brave and noble deeds to justify the hope and pride the old couple had in him. When the boy reached his teen years, the age of the long fast, Grey Falcon was determined that his son should surpass all others by seeing a vision from the spirit world. This would be a source of strength for the remainder of his days. To achieve this goal, White Beaver must fast for a longer period than that hitherto undergone by any boy of the tribe.

To prepare the lad for the twelve-day ordeal, the old man took him to the sweat lodge. Here he endured the steaming heat for as long as he could. Then he dashed out and plunged into the cold river that flowed nearby. Several times he repeated this procedure. Then Grey Falcon took the branches of a cedar and scrubbed his son's body until the blood ran. White Beaver was ready now for the twelve-day fast, during which, having attained purity of body and soul, he would receive the vision from the spirit world.

With hopes high for the successful outcome of the boy's long vigil, Grey Falcon led his son to the lodge that he had built for this occasion in a remote part of the forest. Here, he left the boy.

Every morning, Grey Falcon visited White Beaver. He reminded him of the honour and glory that would be his if he endured the fast without complaining. For seven days, the boy lay without motion on the mat prepared for him, and was sustained by the encouraging words of his father.

On the eighth day of his fasting, he raised imploring eyes to his father, and, in a voice made weak by suffering, said, "Father, give me some food now. I dreamed that some evil would befall me if I continued to fast longer." But the father, anticipating the pride that would be his when his son excelled all others, reminded him that only a few more days of his fast remained.

For two more days, the boy lay motionless; so faint was his breathing that his soul might already have begun its westward journey. Then, on the eleventh day, he once more whispered his request, "Give me some food now."

But Grey Falcon replied, "Keep up your courage, my son, you who have endured so much. Surely, a vision will be revealed to you this night. Only one more day remains; then you shall have all the food you want."

The twelfth day, even before the sun had emerged from under the cloak of night, Grey Falcon approached the hut. His heart quickened and he stopped abruptly: he could hear the sound of White Beaver's voice talking to someone within the hut. For the first time, he had a foreboding that all was not well. In fear and apprehension, he silently drew nearer to the hut and cautiously peeked through a small opening.

His startled eyes beheld White Beaver at the far side of the lodge painting his body with red paint. Already, he had covered his breast and was painting his shoulders as far as he could reach. All this time, he talked to himself, "My father will be disappointed. He wished me to achieve fame and renown; instead, he will never look upon my human form again."

Overcome by remorse, Grey Falcon cried out, "Wahbi Ahmik, Wahbi Ahmik, what have I done? What have I done? Do not leave me, Wahbi Ahmik, my son."

Startled, the boy dropped the brush and fluttered to the highest point of the lodge where he perched. He had changed into a robin redbreast. In a soft, reassuring voice, he spoke to his father.

"Though I have changed my form, I will not leave you, Father. You will see me in the forests and fields. It is true that I shall not achieve fame and glory, as you

had hoped. However I shall serve my people in a different way. My bright colour and happy song will gladden the hearts of all who behold me. Each year, when the snows are beginning to melt and the streams to waken, my voice will be the first to proclaim the arrival of spring. My cheerful notes will be a message of hope, a reminder to all men that the Great Spirit still cares for them."

Then, with a flourish of wings, he was gone, his flute-like notes fading away farther and farther into the forest.

## Two Dead Persons

In another legend, the robin's message is not one of good cheer.

For several days, two Ojibway boys had been lost in the forest. Though they had given the boys up for dead, their heartbroken parents still searched for the bodies in order that they might give them proper burial. Wearied and overburdened by grief, they were sitting by the fire when their melancholy was interrupted by the antics of a robin, flitting back and forth from tree to tree repeating this refrain, "Neeshewuk-jeebeyuk, Neeshewukjeebeyuk", which is Ojibway for "two dead persons". After singing this song several times, the robin flew farther into the woods. He repeated his message, as though beckoning them to follow. Realizing that the robin was trying to show them something, the parents followed the bird deep into the heart of the forest. Here they found the bodies of the two boys, who had been dead for some days.

Since that time, the robin, with his message "Neeshewukjeebeyuk", has been respected by the Ojibways.

## How the Birds Got Their Colours

Many of the Indian legends centred about a benevolent deity, such as Gitche Manitou or the Sagalie Tyee, who, in response to the entreaties of his children of the air, squeezed juices from the berries and pounded precious stones into powder to make paints rivalling in brightness the clouds at sunrise, the flowers in summer, and the leaves in autumn. These he put into paint pots and used to tint the birds' feathers.

Of all these legends, the Micmac story of Glooscap and the birds is the most fascinating. It has all the ingredients of a good story: the wicked giant, the plight of children bereft of parents, the kindly intercession of friends, and the happy ending.

Long ago, before the coming of the white man, there lived a wicked giant named Wolf-Wind who roamed up and down the land wreaking havoc wherever he went. Fortunately he dwelt most of the time in a remote cave far, far to the north in the Land of Night. On warm days, when the bright sun looked down on calm waters and a placid landscape, men knew that Wolf-Wind was hiding in his Cave of Winds.[13]

But his spirit, which craved misery and destruction, could not long be still. Aroused by an uncontrollable desire to destroy, he roared out from his cave and stalked the land. At his coming, the trees trembled with fear. They flailed their branches about, striving, in vain, to flee from him, for they were rooted to where they stood. The flowers cowered to the ground trying to escape his mighty onslaught; the waters grew white in terror. Leaping higher and higher, they jostled each other and flung themselves against the

13. Note the similarity to Greek legends of the winds which were locked up in a cave and placed under the care of Aeolus.

rocks that barred their progress.

Made wary by unhappy experiences, the Indians living along the coast seldom ventured far out to sea. They knew that Wolf-Wind often came without warning. On one occasion, however, encouraged by a long period of warm, calm weather and wishing to obtain food for the winter, the grown-ups both men and women, left the children alone on shore while they put out to sea to fish. They had not ventured far when a dark cloud blocked the sun. The sea, sensing the coming of the giant, stirred anxiously. Suddenly, with a howl, Wolf-Wind hurled himself at the helpless boats, capsizing them, and flinging the occupants to their death in the heaving waters.

Ravenous with hunger for further victims, Wolf-Wind ranged up and down the coast in search of the children. He knew they would be helpless victims, since he had killed their parents. But the children had heard him as he came screaming towards the land, and hid themselves in a cave. After pushing a rock in front of the entrance, they cowered in a far corner while Wolf-Wind hurled himself again and again against the boulder. Only as morning approached did he weary of his efforts. Then, screaming an oath that he would kill them another day, he swept along the shore, dashing the waves against the rocks and uprooting the trees that stood in his way.

Long after Wolf-Wind had gone, the children remained huddled in the cave. Their immediate concern was to seek shelter of the trees, whose leaves seemed to beckon them and offer assurance of a haven. At last, they ventured out. Far into the forest they wandered until they came to a valley nestled among the shoulders of two high hills studded with trees. A stream meandered beneath willows whose

overladen branches dipped into the waters. Here, under cover of the forest, far from the reach of Wolf-Wind, the children found shelter.

However their peaceful sojourn was to be but an interlude. True to his word, Wolf-Wind ranged up and down the forest, searching relentlessly for them. No cave was too remote, no valley too secluded, to escape his scrutiny. But the trees with their thick cover of leaves succeeded in hiding their young friends. Screaming with rage and frustration, Wolf-Wind retreated to the northland, leaving a path of death and destruction behind him, and vowing to destroy the trees.

Later, on a moonlight night when the stars looked down on the sleeping forest, he resumed his search. This time, instead of announcing his arrival in his usual boisterous manner, Wolf-Wind approached the forest stealthily. At his side was another giant who had with him a strange charm—the Charm of the Frost. So powerful was this charm that the leaves of the trees, one moment green and vibrant with life, were, the next moment, transformed by death into waxy yellows and scarlets. Unhinged from the trees, they drifted down and coloured the forest floor.

Wolf-Wind flung himself at the forest. He shook the branches until they were completely bare of leaves. Then he was ready to pounce upon his prey. However the sturdy Fir, Spruce, Pine, Hemlock, and Cedar had originally come from the far, far north, and were immune to the Charm of the Frost. The children gathered beneath their branches, secure in the comfort they offered.

When they saw what Wolf-Wind had done to their tree friends who had protected them for so long, the children were sad. Summer had departed for the south and the northern land was barren and lonely. Soon winter came, covering the bare branches and bleak ground with a mantle of white. Glooscap, as was his wont at this time of year, visited his people to give them comfort and assurance. Arriving in his huge sled driven by his faithful dogs, he greeted the children and asked them what gift they wished. Thinking only of their tree friends who had sheltered them in their time of need, they replied, "Bring back to life the leaves that the wicked giants from the North have killed."

Glooscap gazed down upon the children. Thoughtfully he puffed away on his long-stemmed pipe. The smoke curled lazily upwards before losing itself in the skies. Then slowly, as though thinking out his ideas, he spoke:

"I cannot grant your exact wish, for it is too late to restore to the bare branches the leaves Wolf-Wind has stripped from them. However I can bring them back to life in a different form. They shall be changed into birds. Not birds like the seagull, the kingfisher, and the loon, whose dwellings are in the watery places and wind-swept shores, but birds of the forest who, remembering that they were born of the leaves of the trees, shall live as close as possible to the branches whence they came. At the approach of winter they will leave for warmer climates, but, when the warmth of spring touches the land, they will return.

"The branches will not always be bare. They, too, will bring forth new life in the spring. Buds and shoots will grow and flourish. In summer they will offer shelter, just as those did whom Wolf-Wind has slain. Each year, Wolf-Wind and the Giant of the Frost will kill them and tear them from the branches, but each spring new leaves will appear."

So saying, Glooscap raised his arm. Immediately

there was a vibrance of rushing wings. Thousands upon thousands of birds rose in shrill chorus, twittering, fluting, and chirping as they fluttered from branch to branch. Their colours were vivid and varied. The warblers and the evening grosbeaks were the hue of the aspen leaves; the tanager, the scarlet of the sumac; the robin and the rose-breasted grosbeak were splashed with the red of the maples.

Then it was winter. The birds did not remain in the northland. They journeyed southwards to join summer in his warm abode. Each year, just as new life stirs within bud and branch, they return to their former home to live amongst the trees that gave them birth, and delight with their songs, the children whom they sheltered long ago, in another life.


## How the Peacock Got Its Spots

To the Greeks, the most beautiful of birds was the peacock with its rich green and blue irridescence. As it proudly spreads its fan of tail feathers, myriads of spots intensify the pageantry of colour. The Greeks thought that these spots, with their inner and outer circles, resembled the human iris and its retina. Here is a legend telling how those many eyes came to be placed on the tail of the peacock.

Zeus, although wedded to Hera, did not focus his attentions solely on her. Indeed, Greek mythology is to a considerable extent a chronicle of his amours with other women, both mortal and immortal. The only deterrent to these extramarital ventures was the jealousy of Hera, whose anger Zeus, though king of the gods, held in the same respect that mere mortal men accord to the wrath of their wives.

One day Hera looked down from Mount Olympus

and saw the earth shrouded in clouds and dense fog. She suspected the worst: Zeus was trying to conceal his amorous activities. Spurred on by jealousy, she pierced the cover of dark clouds. There stood Zeus. A white cow grazed placidly in a meadow near him.

Now, to the uninitiated, this might have appeared an innocent scene, but not to Hera. Had Zeus not transformed himself to a swan when pursuing Leda; to a bull, when wooing the beautiful Europa; and even to a golden sunbeam in order to gain access to the chamber of Danae, mother of Perseus?[14] Ever mindful of Zeus's past conquests, Hera was not to be taken in by this outwardly innocent scene.

Hera's jealous suspicions were, in fact, justified, for her husband had been in the company of Io, the beautiful daughter of the River Inachus. At his wife's approach, the apprehensive Zeus changed Io into a white cow.

Hera, determined that two could play this game of deception, concealed her anger and feigned admiration for the animal, begging Zeus to give it to her as a present.

What could Zeus do but grant her request! A refusal would have been proof to Hera of his guilt. So, with outward grace and inward reluctance, he gave the cow over to her keeping.

Hera immediately hid Io in a remote valley so that Zeus would not find her, and put Argus, a creature with 100 eyes, in charge of her. So watchful was his scrutiny that all 100 eyes never closed in sleep at the same time.

Meanwhile the distraught Zeus summoned his faithful messenger Hermes, and bade him seek everywhere for his beloved Io. After a long and dili-

14. See R.S. Lambert, "Perseus and Andromeda", *Myths, Legends and Fables*.

gent search, Hermes came upon the remote valley and the fine white cow. But he was confronted with the vigilant eyes of Hera's servant, Argus! How could he release the cow from the custody of a guard with 100 eyes?

Hermes devised a plan. Disguising himself as a shepherd, and taking with him his pipe of reeds, he entered the valley and began to entertain the lonely guard with stories and songs. Now, whether the stories were boring, or whether there were too many of them, Hermes's purpose was accomplished. One by one, the heavy-lidded eyelids of Argus drooped in slumber until finally all 100 eyes were closed. Immediately Hermes sprang to his feet, drew a sword which he had concealed beneath his shepherd's robes, and with a flourish lopped off the head of Argus.

When Hera heard what had happened, her immediate concern was for the fate of her servant. She could not restore him to life; instead, she took his eyes and placed them on the tail of her favourite bird, the peacock. This is why, to this day, the beautiful tail feathers of the peacock display their hundred eyes.

## Snakes

> The infernal Serpent; he it was whose guile
> Stirred up with envy and revenge, deceived
> The mother of mankind.
>
> Milton, *Paradise Lost*

In most religions and legends, the snake, or serpent, represents the principle of evil.[15]

15. There are exceptions to this prevailing principle. The Greeks often regarded harmless snakes as tutelary deities. A serpent twined around a staff was the symbol of Aesculapius, the god of medical art.

In Greek myths, when Mother Earth wished to avenge the slaying of her giant offspring by Hercules and the Olympians, she gave birth to Typhon, the largest monster ever born, fathered by Tartarus, most dreaded of the rulers of the Underworld. From the thighs downward, Typhon was a coiled serpent. His arms, when spread out, reached 100 leagues in either direction. Instead of hands, he had countless serpents' heads. This monster succeeded in driving the Greek gods in terror from their home on Mount Olympus to seek sanctuary in the land of Egypt. It rendered the mighty Zeus himself helpless. Only through the timely aid of Hermes and Pan was Zeus's strength restored to him, so that he was able to snatch final victory out of what seemed certain defeat.[16]

Medusa, the Gorgon, with her hair of coiled snakes, so terrified all that looked upon her that they were literally turned to stone. Perseus, the Greek hero, succeeded in slaying her without looking at her dread countenance. When he was flying over Africa on the winged sandals that Hermes had given him, drops of Medusa's blood fell to the ground below. From her blood sprang the poisonous vipers that inhabit Africa to this day.

Thus, in Greek legend, the snake symbolizes evil, the power of darkness, of principalities opposed to the ruler of the universe. Usually the serpent is associated with Mother Earth, out of whom it emerged. Worship of the female deity was supplanted by that of Zeus and the Olympians, as suggested in the story of Apollo's slaying of Python, the emissary of Mother Earth and of Hera, Queen of the gods.

16. Robert Graves, *The Greek Myths*: II

## Apollo and the Slaying of Python

The divine Apollo, the radiant god of the sun, and his beautiful twin sister, Artemis, goddess of the moon, were the offspring of Zeus and Leto, daughter of the Titans Coeus and Phoebe. Overcome by jealousy, Hera vowed that Leto would not be delivered of child in any place where the sun shone, and to enforce her vow sent the serpent Python to pursue Leto all over the world. Zeus, however, commanded the south wind to help Leto who, borne on its warm wings, escaped beyond the reach of Python. On the Aegean island of Delos,[17] she gave birth to twins, Apollo and Artemis.

Apollo soon became the favourite of his father, who presented him with a golden chariot and white horses with golden manes. Arrayed in his tunic of golden panther skin, his broad handsome brow shining forth beneath locks of lustrous golden curls, his golden bow ready for instant action, he symbolized the beauty and physical perfection of the Olympians.

No sooner had Apollo been given the golden bow and the quiver of golden arrows than he sped from Olympus in pursuit of Python, whom he found on the slopes of Mount Parnassus. Although Apollo wounded him, the serpent succeeded in escaping his pursuer and took refuge in a deep cave at Delphi, the oracle of Mother Earth. Apollo, relentlessly following the trail of blood left by the wounded creature, reached the entrance to the cave, but was unable to enter the narrow opening.

Standing at the cleft in the rock, Apollo removed an

17. In honour of this divine birth, a decree was passed forbidding anyone to be born or to die on Delos. Sick folk and pregnant women are ferried over to Ortygia instead. See *The Greek Myths*: I.

arrow from his golden quiver, breathed on the arrow-head before stringing it to his bow, and sent it speeding like a flash of light into the darkness of the cave. Immediately flame burst forth. A cloud of smoke spiralled from the cave. Again and again, Apollo shot at random into the fissure. Now smoke was pouring forth from the opening and the serpent was forced to crawl to the surface. Here Apollo slew it, skinned it, and kept the hide as a memento of the encounter.

Mother Earth besought Zeus to punish Apollo, not only for the killing of Python, but also for violating her oracle, which was sacred to the gods. To make amends, Apollo instituted the annual games at Delphi which he called the "Pythian" Games, in honour of his adversary.

In Indian legend, too, the snake represented power antagonistic to good. The Ojibways believed that the snake-sturgeon was evil and that whoever ate it would become a snake or would be smothered by snakes. At each end of Lake Hanna, where these creatures had been seen most frequently, were erected offering rocks to the evil snake-sturgeons. Indians travelling across this lake placed gifts of tobacco there so that no harm would overtake them.[18]

The west-coast Indians tell a legend of the "salt-chuck oluk", or sea serpent. A young Indian, in contact with the whites, was so infused by the white man's greed for gold and material possessions that he became an outcast from the tribe. In disgust at his un-Indian conduct, the Sagalie Tyee turned him into a monstrous sea serpent, a creature loathed and

18. Norval Morriseau, *Legends of My People, the Great Ojibway*

scorned by man. The salt-chuck oluk was finally killed by a youth who was loved by all because of his generosity and concern for others. Thus the salt-chuck oluk represented greed, the worst sin the Indians could conceive of. Only goodness and generosity, as symbolized by the noble youth, can stamp out greed among the people.[19]

The legend that best depicts the serpent, or snake, in its role as a force counter to good, is based on fact. It is the story of Hiawatha.

## Hiawatha and Atotarho

For most of us, the name Hiawatha is associated with the hero of Longfellow's poem: he who was born of Wenonah, daughter of Nokomis, who had fallen from the sky, and Mudjekeewis, the West-Wind; he who, Jonah-like, was swallowed by Nahma, the giant sturgeon; he who provided his people with maize, the gift of the Great Spirit; he who finally embarked in his canoe and followed the sunset and the purple mists of evening to the Kingdom of Ponemah, the Land of the Hereafter. Longfellow's Hiawatha is a legendary figure, based largely on the Ojibway myths concerning Nanna Bijou. The real Hiawatha was of the Mohawk tribe. He accomplished a worthy undertaking: the founding of the Five Nations of the Iroquois, the strongest force in Red North America, north of Mexico.

The Master of Life, weary of the wars and bloodshed that were threatening to destroy his Indian children, summoned to a council meeting the warriors of tribes ranging from the Blackfoot, in the west, to

19. E. Pauline Johnson, *Legends of Vancouver*

the Mohawks, in the east. In a voice like thunder, he chided them for their constant strife and warfare; then, in the tone of an indulgent father forgiving his wayward children, he expressed his hope that they would share the lands that he had given them to hunt, the streams abundant with fish, and the marshes filled with wildfowl. He told them that a wise medicine man would be sent unto them, to show them the ways of peace and to live as one of them. If they heeded the medicine man's words, they would multiply and prosper; if they did not, they would fade away as the snows melt before the onrush of spring.

The years passed, and the Indians waited in vain for the promised one to appear unto them. Though a term of peace followed the great council meeting, the tribes soon forgot the warning of the Master of Life and again engaged in savage warfare.

The birth of Hy-ent-wat-ha, the Comber Out of Snakes, whom we know as Hiawatha, was not marked by the blazing of a new comet in the sky or a tremor of the earth. His early life followed a pattern common to that of the youths of his tribe. He grew up with no knowledge of the world other than that part of New York state he had travelled either on foot or by canoe. Yet, as he approached manhood, he increased not only in body but also in spirit. Like all great men he had a dream, a vision that had been implanted in him by the Master of Life. That vision was of a world where wars had ceased, where man was at peace with man, and tribe with tribe, where the spiritual power (orenda) within each individual was strengthened, where mercy, justice, and right living prevailed.

Like all good men, Hiawatha sowed the seed of his ideas in others by the example of his own life. His fame spread not only as an orator who could enflame others by his zeal, and as a medicine man who could converse with spirits, but also as a good man who respected the rights of others and was just towards all. Gradually his ideas took hold of his own tribe, then began to spread to other tribes in the eastern regions of what is now the United States.

However the Master of Life has always to contend with the power of darkness, with the ruler of the Underworld, the force of evil that was born at the same time as the Master of Life. This power took the form of a misshapen creature with claws for hands and feet and with snakes for hair.[20] This was Atotarho, the dreaded medicine man of the Onondagas.

The contest between good and evil: between Hiawatha, destined to become the saviour of his people, and the cunning serpent, Atotarho, began. At first, Atotarho's medicine proved the stronger. Like Job, a series of afflictions beset Hiawatha: his beloved wife, Wanutha, was felled by an arrow wrought by the magic of Atotarho; one by one, his daughters were struck down by the same powerful magic. Alone, and rejected by the people whom he had tried to save but who now doubted his power, Hiawatha wandered from tribe to tribe among the Iroquois, preaching and teaching; now, however, the seed of his ideas fell upon barren soil.

Though the wily serpent by the use of guile may seem to conquer the forces of good and his power spread like thistles in a field, the Master of Life does not forget the good and faithful servant who, like

20. Obvious parallels are the traditional picture of Lucifer with cloven hoofs, pointed ears and tail; the misshapen Hephaestus of Greek mythology, who like Lucifer, was cast out of his heavenly home; and the Gorgon, Medusa, with coiled serpents for hair.

Hiawatha, keeps his face steadfastly turned towards his goal. Just when Hiawatha's need was greatest, a helper was sent to him—a prophet named Degano-weda. Deganoweda, too, had dreamed a dream. His dream took the form of a vision of a great spruce tree—the "Tree that Lights the World". The top of this tree reached through the sky to the land of the Master of Life. Its branches represented the sisterhood of all tribes, and its roots were the five Iroquois tribes. An eagle, perched at its top, kept watch against any enemy that might attempt to break the peace.

As flame sweeps through grasses parched by the heat of the sun, so Hiawatha's zeal, fanned by Degan-oweda's vision of the "Tree that Lights the World" spread to the neighbouring tribes. One by one, the powerful tribes of the Iroquois—first the Mohawks, then the Oneidas, the Cayugas, and the Senecas—were converted to the teachings of Hiawatha and Degano-weda: the union of the Iroquois tribes into a confed-eracy to be called the Ho-de-no-sau-nee was about to be accomplished. The one obstacle to complete union was the Onondaga tribe. It was still under the evil spell of Atotarho.

At this moment, the Master of Life inspired Hiawatha with an idea that was to make the difference between success and failure. Seizing on it as the only hope of success, Hiawatha and Deganoweda ventured once more into Onondaga territory with a message for Atotarho and the Onondagas. After three suns had journeyed across the sky, night found them seated before the council fire of the Onondagas. The light of the campfire revealed only hostility, gleaming like panthers' eyes in the shadows of the night. In the midst of this sinister gathering, his misshapen form further distorted by the ebb and flow of gleam and shadow that seemed to transform him into a thousand different shapes, Atotarho's eyes glared malevolently at Hiawatha. From his head, snakes twined and intertwined their glistening lengths, their eyes darting forth pinpoints of cold white light. As Hiawatha stood up to address the gathering, he was the centre of a host of hostile eyes. The only warmth in all that grim circle was the reassuring nod of Deganoweda.

Hiawatha spoke, his firm, strong voice shattering the silence of the night. With words as vivid as the scarlets and reds of sumac and maple in the autumn forest, he painted scenes of carnage, of wanton destruction and useless slaughter caused by the cruel hand of brother turned against brother in the conflicts that had been spilling the lifeblood of the Iroquois tribes until their very survival was at stake. He reminded them of the gathering strength of their ancient enemies, the Algonquins, who soon would be able to break the separate Iroquois forces as easily as a dry twig is snapped as tinder for fire.

Then, with an eloquence that could only have been inspired by the Master of Life himself, Hiawatha told of Degonaweda's vision of the "Tree that Lights the World". His words quivered with the zeal of his own faith, as he outlined the organization of the Ho-de-no-sau-nee, the League of the Five Nations of Iroquois tribes that would not only make wars to cease among the brother nations but also be the rock on which to build a wider union, a union joining in hands of peace all the tribes from the eastern sea to the mountains of the sunset.

He explained how the council of the League would be made up of fifty sachems from the five tribes. Since women were the source of life, since to them was entrusted the rearing of the young child, and since they were most vitally interested in preserving peace, the matrons of the tribes would be entrusted with the responsibility of choosing the sachems. Because the Onondaga village was located in the centre of Iroquois territory, it would be the meeting place of the council and the Onondagas would be the Keepers of the Council Fire, a fire that would burn forever as a symbol of the light of peace.

Then came Hiawatha's final revelation: whether it was inspired by the Master of Life or the subtle influence of the powerful medicine of Atotarho, no one knows. Atotarho, chief medicine man of the Onondagas, was to be the Chief Sachem!

As the branches of the aspen bow and rustle their leaves before the breeze, so the Onondaga leaders huddled in excited consultation. Then all eyes were fixed upon Atotarho as he uttered these words: "We accept these terms. We shall join our brothers in the Ho-de-no-sau-nee. We shall be the Keepers of the Sacred Fire."

Runners were despatched to the other tribes. The leading men of the Five Nations assembled at the Onondaga village for the ceremony that was to inaugurate the formation of the Ho-de-no-sau-nee. Solemnly and with impressive ceremony, as is the Indian custom, the fifty sachems were installed into office. There remained only the crowning of Atotarho as the Chief Sachem.

Holding the sacred antlers that were the symbol of office, Hiawatha with slow and measured tread advanced to the front of the assembly where Atotarho waited expectantly. As he raised the antlers above Atotarho's head, he intoned these words:

We do now crown you with the sacred emblem of the antlers, the sign of your lordship. You shall now

become a mentor of the people of the Five Nations. The thickness of your skin shall be seven spans, for you shall be proof against anger, offensive action, and criticism. With endless patience you shall carry out your duty, and your firmness shall be tempered with tenderness for your people. Neither anger nor fear shall find lodgment in your mind, and all your words and actions shall be marked with calm deliberation. In all your official acts, self-interest shall be cast aside. You shall look and listen for the welfare of the whole people and have always in view, not only the present but the coming generations—the unborn of the future Nation.[21]

At the very moment the crown of antlers was placed on Atotarho's head, a gasp of amazement broke from the assembled multitude. No sooner had Hiawatha's hand brushed against Atotarho's hair than the snakes fell to the ground, twisted in convulsive movement, and then shrivelled and died. Atotarho's misshapen body was transformed into a handsome, upright figure. His animal claws changed into the hands of a man.

Thus evil had yielded to the force of good, and from that day forth Atotarho, as Chief Sachem, devoted himself to furthering the cause of peace among the Five Nations. Hiawatha, the "Comber Out of Snakes", as he was henceforth known, spent the rest of his life spreading the cause of peace and the brotherhood of man to nations beyond the Iroquois confederacy. In his sacred white canoe, he carried the message to tribes far into the interior of the continent. Though his words failed to accomplish their purpose, he continued his efforts until the day came when he embarked

21. The oath of office, as set down in the Constitution of the Iroquois

in his canoe on the voyage whence he never returned.

As Hiawatha journeyed towards the setting sun, Gadowaas, the Soul-Keeper, took, from his wampum belt, the most brilliant star—which we call the Milky Way—and fastened it to Hiawatha's belt to light his path. Thus, Hiawatha reached the land beyond the sunset and the stars where peace ever dwells and all the children of the Master of Life live in harmony in deep meadows and flowery forest glades set in a summer sea.

To this day, two seats are left vacant at the council meetings of the Iroquois: these are reserved for Hiawatha and Deganoweda, whose spirits still guide the deliberations, ever counselling the ways of brotherhood and peace.

# 5
# The Quest

When the Greek hero Perseus attained manhood, he was visited in a dream by a lady, tall and beautiful. She wore a helmet, carried a spear and a brightly polished shield, and spoke to him these words:

> Perseus, I am Pallas Athene. I know the hearts of men. From souls of clay I turn away, and they are blest, but not by me. They fatten at ease, like sheep in the pasture, and like sheep, are forgotten when they die. But to the souls of fire I give more fire, and they also are blest, but not like the souls of clay. For I drive them forth by strange paths, that they may fight the monsters, the enemies of gods and men. And some are slain in the flower of youth, no man knows where or when; and some win noble names, and a fair and green old age. Tell me now, Perseus, which of these two sorts of men seem to you the more blest?

Perseus answered:

> Better to die in the flower of youth, striving nobly, than to live like sheep and die unrenowned.[1]

1. Charles Kingsley, *The Heroes*

Whereupon Perseus was commissioned by Pallas Athene to set forth in quest of Medusa, the Gorgon. Medusa was a monster who, instead of hair, had serpents coiling about her temples. Her eyes were so cruel and terrible that all who looked upon her were turned to stone. Once Perseus had found this evil creature, he was to accomplish the seemingly impossible task of slaying her.

In spite of the dangers and obstacles that beset him, Perseus set about his mission zealously, never for a moment swerving from his purpose.

The story of Perseus typifies not only the Greek concept of the hero, but the heroic *ideal* that has been implanted in souls of fire, in men of diverse cultures, and as far separated in time as the Old Testament and recent science-fiction narratives. The theme of a popular television series, "To seek out new civilizations and to boldly go where no man has gone before", is as old, at least, as Homer's *Odyssey*. For the hero of either story, these words could apply with equal validity, "Life for him was an adventure, perilous indeed, but men are not made for quiet havens".

On this voyage so fraught with dangers, Odysseus might have been tempted to abandon his goal. On his homeward journey, he had no sooner left Troy than he was driven off course by adverse winds to the north coast of Africa. He anchored his ships in the harbour of an unknown land, and sent a party ashore in search of fresh water. Here they found a beautiful, peaceful country "in which it seemed always afternoon". The inhabitants were the "mild-eyed, melancholy lotus-eaters" (the Homeric counterpart of the flower children) who offered them to partake of the lotus-fruit. The effect of this plant was similar to opium: Odysseus's men dreamt of their wives, their children, and their homes, and preferred this trancelike dream to the reality of challenge and struggle which they must surmount before they reached home and were reunited with their loved ones. However Odysseus rejected the temptation of this life of ease, choosing to strive against the hostility of the gods and the tempest-tossed sea.

Later, Odysseus could have abandoned the struggle by giving way to the entreaties of the beautiful enchantress, Circe, who, infatuated with his handsome physique and intrigued by his invulnerability to her charms, pleaded with him to reign in Aeaea with her. Though yielding for a time to the blandishments of Circe and the pleasant life in Aeaea, Odysseus forsook all this to continue his journey, even though he knew his immediate destination was Hades, the bleak realm of the Dead, the land of perpetual shade. Still later, he could have given way to the sweet enticement of the sirens who promised him foreknowledge of all future happenings on earth. He could have lived a life of perpetual youth with the beautiful Calypso; but, wearying of her charm, he yearned to be on his voyage once again, choosing the challenge of danger, uncertainty, and death to blissful immortality where all the senses were gratified.

At last, alone and friendless, Odysseus reached Ithaca, only to encounter what, to a lesser man, would have been deemed an insurmountable obstacle. Taking advantage of Odysseus's absence, over 100 young princes had swarmed to his kingdom like locusts. Here they were enjoying a life of ease and luxury, battening themselves on his livestock, swilling his wine, and debauching his maidservants. Moreover, each sought to perpetuate his gluttonous existence by marrying Odysseus's wife, Penelope. But she, in spite of the entreaties of the suitors, remained loyal to the memory of her husband.

With the help of his son, Telemachus, and two faithful servants, and abetted by his own cunning, Odysseus triumphed over the degenerate suitors. Soon their carcasses were strewn over the hall like fishes gasping and quivering after having been hauled out of the ocean. Then, and only then, did he reveal himself to Penelope, from whom hitherto he had concealed his identity. Odysseus's quest was over: he was home at last!

"The spirit of man is nomad, his blood Bedouin, and only death possesses the right to bring to an end the journey to which his myth provokes him".[2] According to legend, within three years of his return, the restless spirit of Odysseus chafed "to seek out new kingdoms and to boldly go where no man has been before". This yearning for new adventure, for the life beset by obstacle and challenge has been recreated by Alfred, Lord Tennyson in his poem, "Ulysses".

> It little profits that an idle king,
> By this still hearth, among these barren crags,
> Match'd with an aged wife, I mete and dole
> Unequal laws unto a savage race,
> That hoard, and sleep, and feed, and know not me.
> I cannot rest from travel: I will drink
> Life to the lees: All times I have enjoy'd
> Greatly, have suffer'd greatly, both with those
> That loved me, and alone; on shore, and when
> Thro' scudding drifts the rainy Hades
> Vext the dim sea: I am become a name
> For always roaming with a hungry heart.
> Much have I seen and known; cities of men

2. Laurens van der Post, *The Dark Eye in Africa*

And manners, climates, councils, governments,
Myself not least, but honour'd of them all;
And drunk delight of battle with my peers,
Far on the ringing plains of windy Troy.
I am a part of all that I have met;
Yet all experience is an arch wherethro'
Gleams that untravell'd world whose margin fades
For ever and for ever when I move.
How dull it is to pause, to make an end,
To rust unburnish'd, not to shine in use!
As tho' to breathe were life! Life piled on life
Were all too little, and of one to me
Little remains: but every hour is saved
From that eternal silence, something more,
A bringer of new things; and vile it were
For some three suns to store and hoard myself
And this gray spirit yearning in desire
To follow knowledge like a sinking star,
Beyond the utmost bound of human thought.
This is my son, mine own Telemachus,
To whom I leave the sceptre and the isle,—
Well-loved of me, discerning to fulfil
This labour, by slow prudence to make mild
A rugged people, and thro' soft degrees
Subdue them to the useful and the good.
Most blameless is he, centred in the sphere
Of common duties, decent, not to fail
In offices of tenderness, and pay
Meet adoration to my household gods,
When I am gone. He works this work, I mine.

There lies the port; the vessel puffs her sail:
There gloom the dark broad seas. My mariners,
Souls that have toil'd and wrought, and thought with
me—
That ever with a frolic welcome took
The thunder and the sunshine, and opposed
Free hearts, free foreheads—you and I are old;

Old age hath yet his honour and his toil;
Death closes all: but something ere the end,
Some work of noble note, may yet be done,
Not unbecoming men that strove with Gods.
The lights begin to twinkle from the rocks:
The long day wanes: the slow moon climbs: the deep
Moans round with many voices. Come, my friends
'Tis not too late to seek a newer world.
Push off, and sitting well in order smite
The sounding furrows; for my purpose holds
To sail beyond the sunset, and the baths
Of all the western stars, until I die.
It may be that the gulfs will wash us down;
It may be we shall touch the Happy Isles,
And see the great Achilles, whom we knew.
Tho' much is taken, much abides; and tho'
We are not now that strength which in old days
Moved earth and heaven; that which we are, we are;
One equal temper of heroic hearts,
Made weak by time and fate, but strong in will
To strive, to seek, to find, and not to yield.

"To strive, to seek, to find, and not to yield," these words embody man's perpetual spirit of adventure. They typify the spirit that prompted Abraham to leave Ur, that motivated Moses to seek the Promised Land, and Jason to embark on his journey for the Golden Fleece. In this century, they apply, just as readily, to Scott of the Antarctic, to Thor Heyerdahl, to Sir Francis Chichester, and to the explorers of outer space.

Sometimes the search is not for brave new worlds, but for a rediscovery of elusive and evanescent moments of glory that have lighted our past. Notable examples are: the quest for the lost Atlantis, for the Holy Grail, for King Arthur's capital, Camelot, for the Kingdom of Lyonnesse that disappeared under the sea, and for Homer's Troy. The following story is the Indian counterpart of these journeys to the past.


## The Lost Island

Somewhere in the inner channel of the coastal region of what is now British Columbia, there is an island which juts up from the mist-enshrouded sea. Its crest is crowned with a circle of towering pines. Though sought by many for over 100 years, this island, lying somewhere in one of the lost channels that lead to the Indian people's past, has been seen by none. To this day, it remains unchartered. According to Squamish legend, many have sensed its awesome presence. Some have even seen, stretched on the water before them, the huge shadow of its rocky shore fringed with a crown of firs. But when they turned to behold the substance behind the shadow, there was nothing. The island is there, but the old Squamish chiefs say that, like other glories of the past, it has vanished into the mists of yesterdays.

Like Lyonnesse and the lost Atlantis, the past of the Indian nations assumes a more golden hue with each passing year. This is readily understandable. In the past, the Indian was not confined to the reservation or the life of an alien in the white man's world. The forests, abounding with game, were his to roam; the oceans, rivers, and streams teemed with fish that were his for the asking. He had his tradition and beliefs to guide him, and, until the coming of the white man, knew little of greed and covetousness. Skilled, coura-geous warriors shared the harvest of their strength and resourcefulness with those less fortunate. Skills, such as carving, boat building, and weaving, that are now largely forgotten, then flourished. The world of the spirit was near to man, and the Sagalie Tyee was known to have revealed himself to many a shaman. Seen through the retrospect of time, this was indeed the Golden Age of the red man in North America.

In this world, long before the coming of the white man, there lived among the Squamish a shaman of prodigious power. He possessed not only the ability to manipulate the forces of nature, to converse with spirits, and to see into the future, but also the courage of the mountain lion and the strength of the grizzly. He was completely without fear; his strength, his hardihood, his endurance were known far beyond the territory of his people. Esteemed for years as a leader of his tribe, he should have passed, as a canoe drifts into the still waters of eventide, quietly into an old age of contentment.

But such peace and tranquillity he was not to enjoy. During his waking hours, whether he was feasting with his people or alone in the solitude of the forest, voices spoke to him. At night, his sleep was troubled by dreams. The voices and the dreams told the same dread prophecy. The sun of the red man was soon to decline. Into his world, white men would come in their teeming thousands and transform grove and woodland into mile after mile of lodges made of stone and wood. Accompanying them, would be disease, greed, and strife. Under the white man's influence, the Indians' strength, courage, and resourcefulness would ebb like the moon-chained tides.

For years, this dream haunted the shaman, driving him from the gatherings of his people, the festivities and the storytelling, to seek the solitude of the forest, the quiet of the secluded lake or the lonely mountain trail. Yet everywhere the dream pursued him, until one day his steps were directed up the steep slopes of Grouse Mountain, whose lofty crags look down on the narrow strip of land, miles beneath, that juts out into the salt water.

After days of fasting on the mountain, the shaman was visited by the Sagalie Tyee who took him by the hand and pointed to the scene far below. Then, with a wave of his hand, the Master of Life created a new world between what is now called False Creek and the Inlet. Lodges of wood and stone, innumerable as the stars in heaven, came into being. Long grey lodges stretched forth into the salt water, while farther back the lodges were white and reached upward into the sky. In the blue sea, huge boats moved silently to and fro, as if guided by a giant hand. Then the Sagalie Tyee lowered his arm; instantly, as in a dream, the scene changed and all was as before. Turning to the wonder-struck shaman, the Sagalie Tyee spoke these words:

"You have seen what is to be, what cannot be undone. This is the world of the white man. Robbed of his lands, deprived of his heritage, a stranger in an unfamiliar world, the Indian will lose all his strength and his courage. He will attempt to adopt the white man's ways: his customs, his religion, his language. Emptied of his pride, his fearlessness, his self-confidence, the Indian will become as nothing."

In dismay, the shaman cried out. "O Sagalie Tyee, I am old and my days are numbered. Take my strength, my courage, and my fearlessness. Hide them where the white man can never find them, but give them to my people who will come after me so that their spirit will never break beneath the white man's rule."

Whereupon, having seen the Sagalie Tyee and

knowing what he should do, the shaman came down from the mountain. Without a moment's hesitation, he slid his canoe into the sea, and paddled into the crimson waters of the dying sun. As he paddled, he sang the songs and legends of his people, his voice growing fainter and fainter as he faded from the view of his tribesmen, whose anxious eyes followed him into the distance.

He came to an island whose rocky shore rose high above him; on its summit, was a crown of firs. As the shaman gazed at the island, he felt his strength, his courage, and his fearlessness leave him and drift towards the island and, like a mist, enfold the fir crown and the looming grey rock.

His strength gone, the shaman drifted on the wings of the morning wind to the shore whence he had begun his voyage. To his people waiting there for him, he said:

"My strength, my courage, my fearlessness, I give to those who shall come after me. To those who truly seek, they shall be given."

Then he returned to his lodge and slept. In the morning, when they came to wake him, he was sleeping the long sleep—the sleep that would carry him on the long journey to the past of his people.

And still the Squamish seek the lonely island lost in the mists of some remote channel.